Analysis of the
Second Amendment

&

the Crisis of Gun
Violence: An Essay

TIM I. PEACE

AuthorHouse™
1663 Liberty Drive
Bloomington, IN 47403
www.authorhouse.com
Phone: 1 (800) 839-8640

ANALYSIS OF THE SECOND AMENDMENT
Timotheus I. "Tim" Peace

Published by AuthorHouse 08/02/2018

ISBN: 978-1-5462-0645-3 (sc)
ISBN: 978-1-5462-0644-6 (e)

e-Book can only be obtained through AuthorHouse
https://www.authorhouse.com/Bookstore/BookstoreHome.aspx

Written from 2013 – 2016
Completed in Worcester, Massachusetts on July 27, 2016

Print information available on the last page.

Please direct critique, comments, and correspondence to:
Timotheus.Peace@gmail.com

To the dearest angels of Sandy Hook whose embryo lives were violently truncated in this cruel world, now rendered immortal to sweetly rock eternally in the cradling arms—and, sit in the blissful and everlasting loving bosom—of the Almighty God.

For our Unfettered Enlightenment, Freedom of Thoughts and the Expressions thereof; Conspicuous Pursuit of Inquisitiveness, and our Liberties to Stand by our Just Maxims; we Stand for the Love of God and Country.

THE SECOND AMENDMENT

A well regulated Militia, being necessary to the security of a free State, the right of the people to keep and bear Arms, shall not be infringed.

—THE SECOND AMENDMENT TO THE US CONSTITUTION

Author's Note

This text proves to be a controversial one: both in scope, timing, and sensitivity of the subject matter. This essay was officially concluded on July 27, 2016, with the addition of some addenda up to November, 2017. And, editing, proofreading, citation and proper referencing continued afterward. This work is incredibly time sensitive and the course of time affects its layout and presentation.

As explained in the text, this essay has to be stopped at some point. More events keep rising that threaten to prolong the subject matter being analyzed, and at some point, updates had to be halted and a stop date has to be stamped on the text. This is rather unfortunate.

I chose to write this text on the Second Amendment as an analytical essay by approaching it through—(I) beginning with an introduction, —(II) a social construct that necessitates it, and, the influence of the Enlightenment thinkers on the American Revolutionaries who eventually crafted and consented to the ratification of the constitution. Further, (III) the idea of weapons and liberty, prevalent in the American society is discussed.

Nothing seems more important than describing (IV) the elusive

• • •

intent of the Second Amendment in the Bill of Rights. More so, (V) a case is made against the landmark 2008 Supreme Court decision on *DC v. Heller*, and this argument is augmented by the concept of (VI) *time, law, and morality.* Also, the consequence of the complexity of the amendment on the society is discussed. This is documented in an arbitrary epilogue, (VII) including some saddening data of firearm disasters. Lastly, this essay is finalized with (VIII), a brief conclusion. This essay can be read somewhat nonsequentially. However, the context of each part may elude such perusal. Also, it is equally important to peruse the footnotes thoroughly as much as this text itself.

It is my anticipation that you'll approach this text open-mindedly, carefully, and get to the very end before drawing conclusions—negative or positive.

The concept of objectivity for ages has been a philosophical unicorn. Or, so it seems. But there is such a thing as morality that, when weighed in the balance, the needle of the scale can point towards objectivity.

PREFACE

lthough, I am supposed to scour for arguments presented by propagators of the concept of the right to unrestrained armament, I however, chose not to. For in doing so—taking the prominent authors of these arguments to task, and thereby present my case—I will neither produce an essay nor a book, but a volume.

Furthermore, I also chose not to consult the Founders' or Framers' "intent." After all, it is not in my place to conduct séances. And I am equally *less* interested in other documents such as correspondence between them, their publications in the formative years of the American Republic, or prominent authored works like the Federalists' Papers. I do not need *much of these* to make my case. Of these, I used as few as necessary. And I firmly oppose these in the application of constitutional law. That is, the duplicity of radical originalism.

It is an exaggeration to contend that the Founder's writings provide context to the interpretation of the law.

Law falls within the realms of classical philosophy. And as such, I welcome philosophical analysis.

I am well aware of the language, culture, and politics of the times.

More so, I am not estranged from American history. Nevertheless, only the history of American gun culture and the *law* is worth exploring. Getting into prolonged history, Supreme Court precedencies, and political bashings are tantamount to "much ado about nothing."

From my vantage point, I prefer to approach this essay in terms of ethics rather than history. This is altogether fitting. In straying from this, I'll venture into "historical forensics." For example, in Justice Stevens' dissent in the *Heller* case, alluding to precedence, he noted that

> No new evidence has surfaced since 1980 supporting the view that the Amendment was intended to curtail the power of Congress to regulate civilian use or misuse of weapons. Indeed, a review of the drafting history of the Amendment demonstrates that its Framers rejected proposals that would have broadened its coverage to include such uses.

My point here is not necessarily a criticism; it is meant to demonstrate how the Courts dig into journals, work of history experts, and other academic sources to make their case. This seems to be "historical forensics."

But my fundamental pursuit is one: provide an objective case for the proper interpretation of the most contentious statute in the American constitution. And that is:

> *A well regulated Militia, being necessary to the security of a free State,*
> *the right of the people to keep and bear Arms, shall not be infringed.*

Besides this, and issues surrounding it in terms of justice, nothing else matters. Of course, this contention is opined by one individual. This, nevertheless, neither makes it wrong nor erodes its objectivity. There comes a time when a single individual can inject "common

• • •

sense" into the popular ethos. Further, an individual can be a person or an object of reason.

In this work, I am presenting a number of arguments pertaining to the Second Amendment. Among the most critical ones, are: one, that a "militia" is not a *person*, and, should it be a term that can be applied to a person, then the constitution allows for its regulation by the government. Two, the Second Amendment, as interpreted at this time, violates the sanctity of human life. And if it meets legal purity in the constitution as it is interpreted and applied today, then the amendment is antiquated.

Here, I stressed the inherent attribute of the sacredness of the gift of life, and, I think I fell short of my anticipated emphasis. I introduced the philosophy of *non vita, non libertas*: no life, no liberty. This maxim is central to this work. I introduced some necessary preludes to this effect to make this case: what philosophy guides and influences the Enlightenment thinkers who founded this nation to have left us with such a vague "constitutional-cultural" tradition?

Three, our current understanding of the Second Amendment undermines the government's ability to maintain the requisite authority over the use of force in the state. This is the bedrock of a strong and functional state.[1]

Culturally, as a people, we are hesitant to attune ourselves to this sort of ideal. However, law enforcement officers are victims of excessive proliferation of firearms. While without a doubt the use of deadly force by American law enforcement institutions is unjust, unethical, and paranoid, a very significant *fraction* of discharge of this force, however, are consequent of the paranoia of an armed populace.

Even more so, the "wary" citizens—that is the staunch devotees of the "Second Amendment"—are less concerned that, the Republic the

---

[1] Weber, M. (1918) Politics as a Vocation

Founders have left us as an unfinished pyramid to last for millennia could end up as a failed state.

Four, arms (firearms), the major if not the only controversy of the statute, makes homicide and anthropogenic hazards easier to be perpetuated and is an antithesis to the ethos of modern civilization. And, if the Second Amendment is interpreted correctly today, then it is an immoral law that all moral individuals should agitate for its abolition.

Other things are discussed, too. Why discuss liberty, social contract, and other phenomena in this essay to some detail in the consummation of analyzing an amendment that enumerates the regulation of arms? This is because of the relationship between the government and the people in a society—the American society, and, how the American people perceive their government. It is also meant to explore the philosophies and influences of the men of the Enlightenment era who brought this nation on this continent to experiment democracy.

The power vested upon the government by people must be counterbalanced in some form. And the government must be equally threatened by the ballot in a legitimate peaceful democracy, rather than the bullet, to genuflect to the will of the people.

The personal liberties of others, innocent and armless, in the land of the free and the home of the brave, and their social contract in the context of society not the government, must be elucidated when their lives are endangered by firearms by those who, directly or indirectly, vociferously defend the right to own guns—especially sophisticated weapons—under the guise of self-defense. The domino effect of this stance is savage homicide rate.

Naturally, this work is divided into three parts: the main essay, a succinct "case against *DC v. Heller*. *DC v. Heller*" which is not the only ruling or precedent set by either the High Magistrate or lower Courts. But as observed by one of the litigant attorneys, after the case:

America went over 200 years without knowing whether a key provision of the Bill of Rights actually meant anything... [N]otwithstanding what amounts to a national consensus that the Second Amendment means what it says: The right of the people to keep and bear arms shall not be infringed. Taking rights seriously, including rights we might not favor personally, is good medicine for the body politic, and Heller was an excellent dose.[2]

This statement, however skewed, points to this case as being the most historically significant Second Amendment case. And, besides its historical significance, the case is also the latest in a chain of disputes over the Second Amendment and conflicting local governments' laws with it. The opinion delivered with its ruling displays the most fundamental problem of the interpretation of the amendment: politics.

Lastly, a dilemma over data concludes this essay as an arbitrary epilogue. The subject matter being addressed by this essay is sensitive and temporal—like an ever-going live documentary, but at some point, writing about it must stop while the docudrama continues with the hope that, peace will prevail over chaos.

---

[2] Neily, C. (2008, August 8). District of Columbia v. Heller: The Second Amendment Is Back, Baby. Retrieved July 29, 2016, from http://object.cato.org/sites/cato.org/files/serials/files/supreme-court-review/2008/9/hellerneily_0.pdf

INTRODUCTION

December 12, 2012 was a pivotal time in American history. And many looked to the government—its elected delegates—to take a symbolic action in canonizing Newton, Connecticut, as a place that marked a turning point in American history: Concord, Philadelphia, Seneca Falls, Birmingham and Selma and so on. But it did not. Many of the parents of the victims of Sandy Hook rightly sought meaning and redemption of America's ailment from their children's sacrifice at the altar of a radicalized version of the Second Amendment that seldom can be curtailed. They, as well as the tearful president and some senators, were helplessly and hopelessly disappointed.

The nation, at least those concerned, bemoaned their democracy, as they see the National Rifle Association tumbled and stifled the president's driven initiative, and intimidated Congress to numbness as the organization perturbed the safety of the seats of its members.

Mass shooting has become so rampant and ubiquitous in the United States, that, its frequency with the rollout of the twenty-first century, is an abomination to civilization. And while mass shooting is not a new phenomenon in the history of this country, the increasing vulnerability and victimhood of juveniles bring the issue to a whole new level.

However, the fact that politicians—both sympathetic and unsympathetic to the issue—seem to be aloof and fettered by powerful lobbying groups, is disturbing in many ways. No doubt, many of the political instruments are individuals of sincere intention, but their vow and devotion to the Second Amendment are mesmerizing, ill-informed, and distorted.

December 12, 2012, may be "a date that will live in infamy", notwithstanding, *many dates have, and will, unfortunately, live in infamy.* From the point of the commencement of writing the manuscript of this essay, to this point (since this text was written non-sequentially), there have been far too many mass shootings—shootings of four or more individuals and other public homicides involving more than one person. The latest being the massacre of nine persons at Umpqua Community College at Roseburg, Oregon on Thursday, October 1, 2015.[3] The event is notoriously senseless as usual. Homicide runs wild. And I can only hope that another won't occur by the time I drop the "pen" or this essay "hits the shelves." This will be left updated.

Today's gun weaponry ethically flies in the face of the Second Amendment
As will be discussed later, the issue of what constitutes arms all Americans are supposedly free to bear is a complicated and twisted semantic issue. Too, many of the Second Amendment devotees are appallingly astonishing in their formidable defense of an exaggerated need for guns. History will not forgive us for our sluggishness in this generation to overturn this infamous societal ethos.

---

[3] Not updated

There is a self-evident sanctity to all human life. This proposition or dogma is fundamental to the constitution—even the Declaration of Independence.

The fact is that the *intent*—and not just "intent" as legal professionals argue as "Framer's intent," but the *intent*—of the amendment as ratified, has been violated by today's savage use of arms. There is no need to construct a language in charitable terms to describe this: America's obsession has descended into outright savagery, one in which in its likeness, some elements of the Dark Ages can be invoked.

It is thus high time that Americans became enlightened as individuals. And in doing so, the barbarism of gun culture with the inclination of demoting the nation to the old Wild West must be eradicated. It is not by any means fair to protest for a "right"—a philosophically prejudicial right—that may deprive others of the ultimate and irreplaceable one.

There are no Second Amendment advocates in the light of these analyses—or potent ones; there are only gun advocates and die-hard effective ones. And these activists argue that gun does not kill people; like one United States Representative Lou Barletta once argued, "Will banning spoons stop obesity?" That is a comical analogy.

Guns, however, kill people—not only the people they are aimed at. Can a person versed in the martial art of 'knife-throwing' spray several knives, spears, or "spoons" at over twenty children and hit one of them several times, almost tearing that fragile body into pieces?

Can a lone knight or a single skilled gladiator achieve this infamous feat?[4]

---

[4] Nineteen people were killed by being stabbed to death—stabbed to death by 26-year old Satoshi Uematsu on Tuesday, July 26, 2016. However, this was in a residential facility that housed disabled individuals. "Mass stabbing" fatalities are extremely rare.

The event at Sandy Hook is an assault on the psyche of American children of this generation. Thus, we need to debate constructively and find a reasonable solution to this predicament so we might "...cherish and achieve a just and lasting peace among ourselves..." Gain a new form of domestic tranquility, and, perhaps, while at it, also gain some international reputation as a domestically decent people.

The Government is complicit

This is the Sandy Hook era, as the Prohibition period ushered in Al Capone's era. The only difference is, there is no constitutional or government imposed "inconvenience" like the prohibition in this Sandy Hook era. No, it's not the Virginia Tech era or any similar savage event; not that the significance or injuries of these are any less significant.

However, the Sandy Hook issue poured the blood of children at the feet of the government, and the government neither found it grotesque nor sacred as it ought to, refusing to mop it. And while decent democracy may raise a clash of opinions, events of this sort ought not to unveil the ugly gridlock of the political machinery of the legislative, executive and the interposition of the Courts.

If it were a foreign terrorist attack by a religious fanatic, it will be a different narrative; everyone will be caught in the fervor of patriotism and geared for war on a foreign soil if called for. But what difference does it make? That is, considering the more or equal barbarity of a domestic terrorist, the like of whom we may see again, and, we have within our powers the ability to curtail or reduce the probability of his terror.

The Supreme Court has taken up a number of cases as pertaining to the Second Amendment and have delivered a number of eye-brow raising rulings, with opinions, unintelligible in argument and in discordant with the constitution that is clear to even to a layperson. It is self-evident—and if not, upon close examination—that what should be objective opinions (constitutionally) emanate from a side of an ideological prism. And, in this case, as with many others, the eyes of "lady justice" is not blindfolded.

More so, it is rather a gross condescension that a government as unwieldy and sophisticated as that of the United States that presides over a nation that supposedly should be the world's greatest democracy can be bought and bullied by a radical lobby like National Rifle Association (NRA).

This is a nation of over three hundred and twenty million people as of this date, with about one-fifth of the global GDP, yet, is five percent of the share of the global population. This is a nation with the most powerful standing military in the history of human civilization. And, this is supposedly the nation with the most sophisticated democracy; perhaps, the nature of this democracy is a problem.

Nevertheless, it is rather ironic that the standing of the sacred stones of the Ten Commandment on the grounds of many states' Courthouses that says, "Thou shall not kill", is passionately defended against secularists who want them removed, by those who simultaneously advocate for unrestricted access to all sorts of ammunition for all.

The Supreme Court is a political Entity

Politics is the instrument by which the democracy of the United States, or any democracy, is expressed. And that the Supreme Court of the United States (SCOTUS) is a political entity is not new in the national consciousness. Notwithstanding, the extent to which it is a political entity is being ignored as a "pink elephant in the room," not being fully acknowledged, known, or understood by the populace and observers.

For instance, it wouldn't catch many academics, in fact, by surprise, to say that associate justices in the SCOTUS have constituents, though not voted into office. Therefore, they act accordingly as to adjudicate cases and *enact policy*, either by eisegetic[5] interpretation of the constitution or judicial originalism, to placate and satisfy their constituencies—in the legislative body, in the executive, and in the populace.

In so doing, they incorporate a dangerous philosophical antithesis to the law—that is, constitutional law—by sometimes, rewriting it, circumventing the requisite process for constitutional amendment. This is not a power vested in the Supreme Court.

So, it was no surprise that when the opinion of the majority was handed down in *District of Columbia v. Heller* in 2008, it was clouded with the fog of political ideology. It was an attempt by the SCOTUS to re-shape a square peg into a round hole, in its harmonizing of that opinion with the constitutional provision.

Sitting on the bench are members who may deny being affiliated with a political party. Some, during congressional hearings for confirmation, may begin to show the world that the exoskeleton of politics will be shed before being fitted with the black robe, only to be cloaked in it.

However, while on the bench, *about all are still affiliated and belong* to a political party (though, society is reluctant to address them as they do, say, with congressional delegates with their political party affiliations). In other words, "let us call a spade a spade."

Nevertheless, their philosophy of justice may evolve or re-evolve during their tenure; hence, we label them by ideology: "conservatives," "liberals" and "swing voters." This is a fundamental proof that justice is neither balanced nor blind. Justices of the SCOTUS, have from case to case and time to time voted along party lines—judges, bound by the rigid twist of ideology and partisanship.

---

[5] Eisegesis: interpretation of Scriptures to fit the reader's devotional or spiritual concerns in a way that describes the interpreter's belief rather than the literal meaning and context of the text.

Congress—polarized, dysfunctional, and impotent it may be for the time being—through check and balances, should restrain the Courts by providing a clear and resolute legislation that interprets the Second Amendment for the greater United States jurisdiction.

While judicial independence is sacred, jurists, especially on the Supreme Court bench do not possess the monopoly on constitutional law, and, they are not exempted, and should neither be exempted, from the federal system of checks and balances. The Supreme Court has been infamous in historically upholding and *creating* immoral law discordant with the constitution or accordant to it. Note that immoral law can be constitutional.

For instance, *Plessy v. Ferguson* is in direct violation of the Fourteenth Amendment and it gave credence and power for the continuance of the violation of the Fifteenth. Roger Taney's opinion on *Dred Scott* was full of vile and malicious comments unconcerned with the constitution. And amidst these many controversial cases, is the interpretation and adjudication of the Second Amendment statute, especially, *Heller*.

The Executive is not enforcing the Law

This is a serious charge to press upon the executive branch of the federal government, the chief of which is the president of United States, and in legal or constitutional matters, his lieutenant, the attorney general of the United States. Nevertheless, this is not new in American history, therefore, the asserted charge is not preposterous.

The executive, sworn to uphold the constitution, has abdicated its authority to unscrupulous agents of states' right. States' right is *often* (and historically) used as a disguise to perpetuate selfish gains and discriminatory ambitions.

The issue of the Second Amendment is an issue of Civil Rights: Civil Rights of Americans who fall victim to gun violence regardless of age, race, sexual orientation and religion.

● ● ●

It is worth understanding, and impressing upon the national consciousness, *that no state has the right to interpose itself between the federal government and its lawful action to defend the rights, privileges, and immunities of a citizen of the United States.* And all constitutional protections of the civil liberties of a US person are within the *original* jurisdiction of the executive—the federal government—to enforce.

Pursuant to statutes of the constitution, states' rights take a back seat to the rights of a citizen or resident of the United States. The federal government—the executive specifically—has all constitutional powers to protect the rights of all the residents of the United States and those subject to its jurisdiction in this manner without restraint. And chief of these rights, is the fundamental liberty entwined with life. Freedom to live, in fact, living not as though merely existing, is literally the lifeblood of a citizen's liberty.

States' rights are limited when a state enacts laws that dictate the civil liberties of the citizens of the United States, most especially, restriction of it. There is a greater exception, noble in fact—when a state expands the scope of civil liberties—chooses to uphold moral law, non-prejudicial and consistent in a non-evasive way, even transcendent to the US constitution, such as the states that prohibited slavery before the United States constitution did. Civil liberties begin with the right to live.

In comparison, there are states with reasonable and landmark gun control measures that the Court's decision in a single case can overthrow.

The right to life transcends the Second Amendment. And the Second Amendment does not necessarily conflict with the fundamental laws and values of the United States. Simply, many people, states, and politicians have radicalized it to the point of religiosity and a deliberate rationalized disregard for the sanctity of human life.

As far as individual rights go, there is no equivocation in the Fourteenth Amendment: *all* individual rights are protected by the federal government—the sacrosanct element constitution of the United States—especially life and liberty that again, transcends anything that can be labeled as "rights." This is altogether moral and just.

And in reference to the Fourteenth Amendment, it can be as well applied to the Second as it was applied it to the First to rescue it from fatuous state agents. The "Establishment" and "Prohibition" clauses of the First Amendment had been evaded by states until the enactment of the Fourteenth.

The same Fourteenth Amendment can firmly bring the "regulation clause" (as will be discussed) under federal domain.

States have found loopholes in the constitution to perpetuate infamous events like Jim Crow, voting fraud, deprivation of Civil Rights based on ethnic background for decades after these were declared illegal by the constitution of the United States. Yet, many representatives of the executive sat idly by without enforcing the constitution which they took an oath to uphold, litigating unnecessarily the rights already enumerated in the document held sacred by the Republic.

The federal government has been nearly neglectful in utilizing its maximum and rightful powers to protect the liberties and immunities of its citizens. Those who reside in *"war zones"*[6] of the inner cities and city outskirts, who are neither criminals nor gangsters, fall victims to bullets. Also, children in suburban schools who get psychopathic visitors with firearms, and nonviolent day-to-day students on college campuses, too, have suffered the injuries and affliction of the government's do-nothingsm.

The states have, with "sword and armor effect,"[7] always found

---

[6] As of June 20, 2016, over 1,800 firearms incidents have been reported in Chicago, Illinois; 200 of them, fatal. Some of the victims of these fatal shootings were teenagers who died from stray bullets.

[7] "Sword and armor effect" refers to the practice of antiquities in which weapon makers advance more sophisticated devices while

loopholes in federal statutes in a shameful attempt to circumvent the constitutional provisions. Also, they have deliberately perpetuated such incursion into the "legal domain" of the federal government, while the federal government stands indolently by, thereby, abdicating its prerogative to execute the statues of the constitution.

In fact, the cry of "states' right" has borne the stamp of an emblem of division and bigotry, both historically, and probably for posterity.

Agents or political actors within a state in this Union who obstruct constitutional justice by interposition should be subjected to prosecutorial actions by the executive branch of the government. Every chief of this office has sworn or affirmed to uphold the constitution of the United States upon the assumption of its leadership.

A formidable lobby in the government's throat

The National Rifle Association has come to represent many things. But the worst of it is its power of interposition between the people and the government—in the form of standing between an electorate/constituent and its elected government officials.

It has by the virtue of the immensity of its political power and leverage, hijacked the machinery of *the government of the people, by the people and for the people.*

It has another form of interposition: standing between government officials—say, in Congress, very intertwined with political ideology, as they attempt to hatch out a legislative approach to combat the issue of firearms violence.

A final form of interposition is when it stands between the three separate arms of governments. When the NRA is able to muster enough power, money, and influence to block the legislative branch

---

armor crafters keep up their design to withstand these designs.
The cycle perpetuates.

from working with the executive, as all forms of its capabilities of interposition, it violates a fundamental tenet of democracy.

The NRA may present a myriad of statements of purpose or mission, but it is simply an organization existing to extract dollars from blood and bullets. And its profiteering exploits is done not only with political intimidation, but intimidation of anyone on their way. Nothing softens the individuals in its tent.

It's almost akin to challenging a mob and ending up in witness protection. For if the Sandy Hook event wouldn't make NRA flexible, and not only that, but will still in the face of that event threaten—by frightening their constituents with inundations of political innuendos— the elected officials who are willing to set aside ideology and pass common sense law, then, the organization's lust for money and blood is unfathomable.

Further, the NRA represents a "clean" form of Al Capone's cabals. Unfortunately, it cannot be "canned" for tax evasion, like Capone. Even if it can be tamed, it seems seldom can it be done, by an elected person, or persons selected by an elected person except for such individuals with an exceptional bravado we are yet to see.

Misplaced loyalty and even infamous sentiments—that threaten their government vocations—have made cowards out many politicians.

The NRA is an emblem of lobby groups affluent enough to purchase democracy and shush government officials or render them impotent. The cabals of this fraternity know no moderation.

A Novel Dimension of Liberty

The survey of the concept of liberty and life in this essay is to explore the ideals that culminated into the Enlightenment thought—that shaped the Founders' ideology—that the blood of tyrant and patriot both need to serve as deterrence to despotism. But should we subscribe to such enthusiasm or hesitance of shedding blood needed for the successful thriving of intra-social and inter-social liberty?

In other words, why is the need for the right to bear *arms* and *civil militarism* sewed into the fabric of American democracy, if that is what the Second Amendment implies?

The novel dimension here is, as it will be reiterated, liberty, like life, is *not* a right. Liberty can be viewed as an imaginary organ every individual is born with and maintains its function as long as life sustains it.

It is the hard currency equally and inherently vested in the human race *recognized* by a liberal society as each's legitimate possession and a legal tender with which the goods and services of *rights* can be negotiated.

Liberty is inherent. It only needs to be recognized by a free society. And once recognized, an individual can bargain and negotiate for negative and positive rights.

Even if jailed or usurped, liberty is still within the living, it's simply unrecognized whether by the jailor in retribution or by an unjust society.

As far as liberty is concerned, one can only bargain or protest for its *recognition*, not negotiate for its *bestowal*.

Non vita, non libertas

With liberty analyzed this way, it can be of no utility without life. American steadfast devotion to an antique law and misinterpretation of it has undermined the value of life.

Liberty should not be taken away by a musket ball, or, a miniature rocket spinning off a projectile.

The victimization of any individual to a firearm incidence, for no reason, senseless reason, irrational reason, avoidable reason, and so on, *permanently* deprives an individual of his life, which sustains his liberty, and, his liberty by which he claims all his lawful rights, and the many more privileges and immunities he can enjoy in his life span.

To say this is unjust is an understatement. Any description of this will be an understatement.

LIBERTY AND WEAPONS[8]

Human liberty, with weapons attached, is a concept and a philosophy predicated upon the assumption, and a fact, that other humans hold the power to exert usurpations over others. Whether it is a lord of a fiefdom, the chief of a village or an "alpha-individual" in the community, the organization of the human species as social entities gives rise to a form of government.

And these forms of governments warrant activism of individuals who want to control their own destinies. Therefore, the possession of lethal ammunition serves as a deterrent against an incursion of a despotic ruler: a form of a "social scarecrow" *in* an individual's private sphere. But this construct is largely theoretical.

In this sense, the very fundamental tool that has evolved with social settings of humans or an individual is offense and defense. Offensive and defensive measures, therefore, warrant the use of weapons. And

---

[8] I have formulated my own ideas of liberty and social contract as I believe should govern a modern free society. Then, I incorporated them with the philosophies of the Enlightenment thinkers. In addition, here, I have attempted to use my analyses to broaden the scope of the Enlightenment philosophy of government fitting for this generation.

• • •

sometimes, to "permanently" lift the burdens of a barrage of despotism, the concept of the threat against *the recognition of* liberty by a society thus calls for the presence of lethal weaponry at an individual's disposal— that is the individual who will "live free or die." How is this construct justifiable in twenty-first century America?

Weaponry, as much as history has demonstrated its efficiency as a bulwark against tyranny, has also led to more anthropogenic events— perhaps, far more or about the same as disease, pestilence, and also, human deaths by famine.

Therefore, a civilized society begs for a balance and moderation. Weapons, as their sophistication increase, have led to their use not only for the cause of inoculation against fettering of humans, but as means to do so, and not only that, to maliciously rob other individuals of their freedom for less than significant objectives.

The credo of many free societies is "liberty or death" as "risk of life and limb"; or a form of self-immolation in defiance of tyranny. Something akin to Algernon Sidney's 1659[9] "Manus haec inimical tyrannis ense petit placidam sub libertate quietem" as a defiant proclamation of an individual's self-determination. Or its American (Massachusetts) derivative: "ense petit placidam sub libertate quietem"[10]: a proclamation of lethal defense of the self-determination and *tranquility* of the peoples of a free society.

These are the rhetoric of the "sons of liberty" romanticizing arms in rhapsodic proportions. If liberty and sword are mutually inclusive, then the sword might actually jeopardize liberty in one way or another— especially among individuals in a common civil and liberal society.

---

[9] Algernon Sidney is an English philosopher who opposed the "divine rights of kings." He will later be executed for his controversial writings, some, central to the American Revolution.

[10] An expression later incorporated in to Massachusetts State's seal.

The heirs of freedom may rue the errors of wielding the sword when in the defense of liberty, the sword becomes an instrument of its destruction. The swords that wage the battle of democracy can equally plunder it into anarchy.

So, what is liberty? An *individual's* liberty can be narrowed simply to self-determination. Too, the *collective* liberty of a group of people can be described in terms of geopolitical, racial, ethnic or religious commonalities—this is important in these analyses. There are, however, some critical dimensions to liberty.

One, *its* fundamental premise is life, so one can adequately say, liberty is inextricable bound to life as characterized by the philosophy of *"non vita, non libertas"*—no life, no liberty. Two, liberty is not only individualized, as much as there is inter-social liberty—the liberty of a group within other groups, there is *intra-social* liberty, that is, the liberty of individuals within a social setting.

Humans are social species, so the second imposes limitations on *absolute* self-determinism and *reduces* it to a "right." And these rights, are predicated upon a social contract.

This is similar to the idea presented by David Hume as *Original Contact*.[11] We must sacrifice some of our "absolute rights" in our inherent liberty (as argued here) to enjoy a civil society.

Three, in both intra-social and inter-social liberal pursuits, the "social" implies that, in human societies, there is invariably human leadership/government. The need for this government to maintain intra-social social contract, and inter-social liberty, dictates that it *must* control power and monopolize the use of force.[12]

Without such reasonable monopoly, a social contract is doomed to collapse, and though inter-social defense of liberty may be formidable,

---

[11] See reference 33

[12] Max Weber: this concept will be espoused further

it will be highly chaotic. These premises are vindicated by some of the characteristics of failed states.

Four, thus in a social contract, with the proclivities of human government towards oppression and despotism, the fairness of this social contract and construct is a measure of *the recognition* of individual liberty *and its bargaining power for rights* in a society. And in entering into this contract, civilians must be "demilitarized" by the regulation of arms-bearing. The reason being, there are other people with precious lives within the *social contract*.

Liberty and Self-determination: Life, Social-Contract, Intra-Social Liberty, and Inter-Social Liberty

LIFE

Liberty, mutually inclusive with the fullness of life, might as well equal life itself. And some philosophers, observers, and so on, will argue,[13] that an oppressed life is no, or, barely *life*.

However, it is *life* in some form as long as an individual is not "functionally" and "medically" dead. Furthermore, to what value an existence is, is defined by that person who is existing, and such definition is what conditions underscore living—in this case, in social settings.

Life matters in the evaluation of the right to bear and keep arms. This is fair to say because weapons are designed to maim and kill—that is, deprive a human being of life. The fundamental liberty and ultimate right of every individual are the "right" to live.

In this sense, full living without the outward hindrance or interference of human instrumentalities to the physiologic and psychological elements of life and living is liberty.

Simply put, liberty *cannot* thrive without life, and life *cannot fully* thrive without liberty.

---

[13] As *I* do contend

• • •

4

Therefore, when a person is killed, either by a state prejudicially, or, for its claimed justifiable right to use life deprivation as a capital punishment, or by a fellow individual; a human being has been robbed of his "total right" and liberty of life.

In fact, life *transcends* a right. It is *more* than an inherent freedom.

No wonder Thomas Jefferson wrote as the preamble to the Declaration of Independence, that "...We hold these truths to be self-evident that all men are created to be equal; and are endowed by their Creator with certain inalienable rights, among these are life, liberty, and the pursuit of happiness..." However, from the philosophical argument presented here, it is noteworthy to mention that liberty gives rise to right, not the other way around.

Rights are available to an individual already endowed with liberty, in a society where such endowment is recognized. Thus, the Declaration's credo is an understatement.

Though liberty is inherently endowed, it is up to a just government of the state—a free and liberal society, to *fully* recognize it in a way that no *one else's* is jeopardized.

On the other hand, the quoted Declaration creed has a number of connotations that can be used to build a set of assumptions: one, there are certain "truths" that are "self-evident"—"rigid" maxims to human existentialism.

Two, that there is a measure of the value of life; all "men" having it at equal value. For instance, all cars, ostentatious or not, are entitled to the same road; a modest or worn out car will occupy the same position is traffic. While this is not a proper analogy, we can all agree that: as far as civil liberties go, *there are no golden lanes for luxurious cars*.

Three, life is "endowed", and that endowment is a treasured entity. Four, though mutually inclusive, life and liberty are two separate entities: one can have a life with unrecognized liberty, but alas, not the other way around. Lastly, life and "the pursuit of happiness" (which is a crucial element of life and liberty) are separate entities, too.

There can be a deprivation of "the pursuit of happiness" and liberty (by its unrecognition) from life. However, those two entities are impossible without life. Hence, life is human's fundamental "endowment" and "freedom" under any social arrangement.

Let's examine these four extrapolations from the excerpt from the Declaration of Independence. The Declaration argues for some form of "social arrangements" drawing its rightness and legitimacy from the "laws of nature and Nature's God." And in a social contract where human interaction exists with an exerting and legitimized body of arbitrators, an individuals' existence is limited to a right within a construct or confines of liberty.

Hence, life—existence—is sacrosanct.

There are "self-evident truths" about life
There are "self-evident" truths, the Declaration argues, within which all are guaranteed "certain inalienable rights" summarized as three fundamental phenomena. These *truths* also demonstrate that these rights are inalienable. There are also certain social phenomena that are "rights", nevertheless, not necessarily mandatory functional part in the mechanics of liberty. This is not because they are not enumerated in the Declaration.

However, life is the very machinery of liberty. Life is invariably, inextricably, and mutually inclusive with liberty. Although in a social setting, it is reduced to a "right," but a "right" it might be, it is the stem upon which all other "certain" and "uncertain" rights sprout and blossom.

To rightly put it, life is the root upon which the stem of liberty sprouts. And liberty is the stem upon which the flowers of "rights" blossom.

More so, the preservation of life trumps infliction of "cruel and unusual punishment," which many jurisdictions within the greater jurisdiction of the United States have validated by making some punishments "usual": by frequent and ubiquitous use of these, and humanization of cruelty.

No better example of states' gun laws violates life like castle laws: cruel and unusual.

The Declaration, being issued at a time when there are no significantly binding international laws, anchored its argument on the principles of nature—not only nature but "Nature's God."

A fundamental rule of Nature's God is "Thou shall not kill." Moreover, in the dynamics of *nature*, normal human emotion—that is, what is characterized as "human nature"—impedes cruel and senseless deprivation of another human's life. Individuals that defy this logic to the extremity are termed "psychopaths." Unfortunately, life deprivation is now "usual", yet cruel, in this so-called civil society.

Therefore, these "self-evident truths" hold in all respects, the value, the uniqueness of life, and the immorality of its deprivation.

Lastly, certain things seem twisted in the contention of lawful and moral regard of life as a fundamental of liberty and its value *as a right*. To clarify this, life is an intrinsic possession "reduced" or described as a "right" within the confines of social contract. This, however, does not diminish the sanctity of life in any way.

Nevertheless, the three *dicta*—life, liberty and the pursuit of happiness—are sequentially "founded" with life being the foundational slab of liberty, and liberty, the supporting slab of all that the "pursuit of happiness" has to offer.

This liberal allegory paints a picture of a pillar or pyramid of freedom, welfare, and self-determinism; all of which are baseless without *life*.

There is a measure of the value of life
Life transcends living it as mere existence. As many would contend, there is a difference between "living" and "existing." Thus, there is a value to life. That all must live it in an "equal" fashion as a "self-evident truth," vindicates this notion. Also, a life lived with restraints on "the pursuit of happiness" is life undervalued.

Gun laws, discrimination, and the value of life
The rural man in Vermont or Virginia, Montana or Mississippi might legitimately want to hunt for game. And while a machine gun is unnecessary for that, his plight is understandable. In proposing any gun laws, this individual might assume that his way of life and cultural upbringing is about to be challenged.

To some, this kind of "gun culture" is taken quite seriously; it is a rite of passage to learn to shoot and to bring home the first hunt. These people are not violent and are not people of the Wild West.

There are also those who enjoy shooting as a recreational activity: sports and shooting range activities as a means of catharsis or leisure, as the case may be. These are all legitimate use of firearms. But, again, simple weapons suffice for these purposes.

Many people have a valid need for self-defense. But the extent to which people arm themselves for defense or security signals an absurdity that there is no existing, or, there is a chronically inadequate law enforcement for their safety and security *in the United States*.

All the aforementioned demographics *tend* to be Caucasians: some economically poor or modest and rural, others relatively economically well off and suburban. These sects constitute the most virulently resistant individuals to any proposal to any change in gun laws even if it means keeping military grade rifles from the hands of lunatics who will turn them on children.

This is how the Second Amendment, the way it is interpreted today, discriminatory. Some lives are undervalued.

Guns in the hands of some economically disadvantaged and rural or relatively economically well-off and suburban Caucasians mostly benefit them. Although, scandals are fairly common.

And the formidable resistance they mount against proposed laws that guarantee positive clarification of the Second Amendment, modest regulation for the safety and security of many citizens, is a critical cause of the illegal proliferation of weapons and firearm possession by the wrong people.

These weapons are a menace in urban areas infested with gang and mob violence, where homicide is unbearably frequent and ubiquitous among many disasters.

Even worse are innocent bystanders, who die by the thousands, standing in the crosshairs of these thugs of war who make daily wages from the fruits of violence. And it is noteworthy to point out that neighborhoods like these are often inhabited by the economically disadvantaged population and minorities, the vast majority of whom, are decent people.

However, these inner-city thugs, despite their mischievous lust for weapons, generally lack the political capital to wage an opposition on a statutory change to the status quo. And if they do, they either lack the sophistication or an iota of willingness to do so. After all, they are criminals. And as such, they both lack legal standing and are seldom interested in lobbying.

This leaves the latter's antagonism as the only conspicuous obstacle and potent war against any progress.

The described rural-urban dichotomous discrepancies and the suburban pleasantries in-between, as described, do not imply lack of rural violence in whatever form they occur. One can point to the rural "sons of anarchy"—both literally and metaphorically, including many extremists organizing as a militia as though they are readying themselves for guerilla warfare. And, too, the "shot out" bikers: Wild West fellas riding on bikes instead of horses.[14]

More so, there are camps of hateful *unregulated* militia: anti-government groups, anarchists, and racists who inhabit compounds that serve as incubators of domestic terrorism. These places serve as breeding grounds of "rational" men and women perpetuating murder—equally as lone wolves—in synagogues, among Americans of African descent both in church, in their homes and on the byways and highways and other minorities and religious groups. Model citizens.

Not only these, there are too many accidental children deaths as a result of firearms owned by careless parent. One of the provisions of the District of Columbia laws, which led to DC *v* Heller, as will be discussed later, would prevent such deaths if it were to be a national statute.

The victims of urban violence, overwhelmingly minorities, poor—regardless of race, age, etcetera, make the status quo of gun laws explicitly and overtly discriminatory by suggesting that all lives are not equal. Whether it is ethnic discrimination as a result of disproportionate ethnic composition in urban population's *de facto* segregation where homicide is astronomical[15], or age discrimination as a consequence of

---

[14] On May 17, 2015, nine people died and at least eighteen people were injured in a shootout between two Waco, Texas bike gangs, which ended with a face-off with the police. One hundred and fifty-one guns were seized.

Martinez, M., Valencia, N., & Morris, J. (2015, December 12). New video shows angle on how Waco biker shootout begins. Retrieved August 02, 2016, from http://www.cnn.com/2015/12/12/us/waco-texas-biker-shootout-new-video/

[15] The Link Between Gun Violence, Race and Politics in America versus US Human Rights Obligations. (2014, April 4). Retrieved August 02, 2016, from http://www.artonissues.com/2014/04/the-link-between-gun-violence-race-and-politics-in-america-versus-us-human-rights-obligations/

lunatics whose fetish is killing children, pupils, and students etcetera: we have declared that *all lives are not created to be equal.*

A society where the liberty of one person is violated in reverence to the liberty of another is a non-liberal, undemocratic, and unfair society.

Life is "endowed"

For whatsoever an individual might subscribe to as the origin of life—creativism, intelligent design, or evolution; life is endowed. Whether it is endowed by God in heaven; or, endowed by nature on earth: life is endowed.

Life is endowed in other ways, too. A parent endows a child, old or young—in an act of procreation—with life. Deprivation of it deprives not only the one whose life has been taken, but also in a way, takes it away from the endower(s).

And this endowed *life*—an ultimate gift—must not be deprived of any individual, unless an individual (in possession of it) poses a *direct* threat to another individual's life.

No person's life should be deprived unless it poses a direct threat to another's; that is, when it presents a "clear and present" danger to another person's life. An individual who *gravely* threatens another person's life have forfeited the sanctity of his life.

How and where is this principle often violated? And, what can violate it? The use of lethal ammunitions—guns—to neutralize individuals that are not necessarily mortally threatening. Guns exacerbate the ease of unnecessary taking of life. In fact, most, if not all, of "castle law" homicides have been perpetuated by firearms. "Castle/stand your ground laws" and the states where these "castle/stand your ground laws" exist have created a societal culture that undervalues life.

Florida, R. (2012, December 14). The Geography of U.S. Gun Violence. Retrieved August 02, 2016, from http://www.citylab.com/crime/2012/12/geography-us-gun-violence/4171/

Life and liberty are two separate entities

As aforementioned, life is the root of the stem of liberty. The Declaration, as penned by its author(s), has a philosophical exposition that underscores "life," "liberty," and the "pursuit of happiness" as "rights." The contention here is that rights are "elements" of liberty. Liberty, being the stem upon which all other *rights*[16] blossom.

One may wonder that the Declaration may as well describe these phenomena as mentioned before, as a three-slab pyramid or three-block pillar, with life at the foundation, then liberty, and the pursuit of happiness—the quality of life, at the apex. Hence, these are rigidly mutually inclusive— "life without liberty is *barely* life" and so on.

However, the principle of *non vita, non libertas* does not necessarily suggest a stance like these. Rather, it describes the fact that when the biological element of it (life) is deprived of an individual, there is no meaning to liberty.

A "hawkish" approach to the Second Amendment to the US Constitution of the right to bear and keep arms, reduces society to a dangerous place. Such that, one individual's right, can permanently deprive another of all possible rights there is—that is, infringement of a person's "total rights"—as liberty imposes.

This risk is the most satisfactory argument that can be mustered, and, opposition to such contention can barely produce a meaningful school of thought. And if it does, it will be a train of politically clouded assumptions, not one founded on morality and "laws of Nature."

Life and "the pursuit of happiness" are separate entities

What does it entail to be happy? Must the basic rights fundamental to a "happy life" come in a "lump"? That is a relativistic question, for "happiness" as used in the day-to-day language is a psychological state of mind.

---

[16] This emphasis is because liberty is eventually reduced to a right in a social setting.

However, liberty in life frees an individual for self-determination in which he may satisfy his "pursuit of happiness" however he finds contentment in it as long as it does not jeopardize other individuals' claim to that same right.

In any case, lethal weapons—unregulated as shall be seen in later sections of this essay—is anathema to life. Such that, the alluded allegorical pyramid or pillar of slabs of rights collapses. And thus, the pursuit of happiness that liberated individuals are free to pursue is defeated.

SOCIAL CONTRACT[17]

Quality of life (what is termed the pursuit of happiness) under liberal principle, with a just measure of self-determination governed by negative and positive rights—is of the utmost importance in any "social arrangement."

There is no intention to explain social contract as it is already known

The government is bound by the rule of law. These laws are often those instituted by the government itself indirectly or directly, to a reasonable degree, by the consent of those being governed.

Likewise, the citizen is bound by the rule of law—laws, somewhat, with mutual agreement with the government, conferring rights, privileges, and immunities to each individual and his neighbor; guaranteed and enforced by a legitimate government in an orderly society not ruled by the entropic chaos of anarchy. These are critical elements of a liberal democracy. A democracy must be impregnated with the ideals of the rule of law.

The fact that *the* individual—or majority of individuals in a free society—does not have an *absolute* "say" or authority over what kinds of law he is bound to obey, has to do with his "neighbor."

Naturally, the right of any given individual must not infringe on the right of another individual. If this were a fixed scientific fact that neither man nor nature can defy, then, a society may be functional without government. And functional in such a way that every individual's liberty is protected, and, co-habitation of humans will not denigrate into an anarchic society.

---

[17] Life, its sanctity, and where ammunitions—it's legal possession and use by the people and the government—fits into this construct discussed here. John Locke's social contract is one of best work of its kind and Max Weber's take on the concept of a state is one of the major philosophies that sustains state-citizenry systems in the world today. In my defense of the sanctity of life and firearms, I have constructed a philosophical framework based on these concepts.

The Second Amendment is expressed with much equivocation, which makes it the most controversial of the ten amendments that survived the shortlisting of the several that were presented as the Bill of Rights. The radical interpretation of it undercuts the fact that one individual's right *must not* infringe on another's.

There may be arguments to this assertion. Is it not the bearing and keeping arms that are meant for the safety of the bearer and keeper? And, does the victim of self-defense deserve a right predicated upon the *infringement*, or more appropriately, *limitations* imposed on the weapon bearer since it is this "right to keep and bear arms" that causes his loss of life?

But there are many counter-arguments to these. Two critical ones are: one, too many gun-related homicides are not a consequence of self-defense, but rather, a nuisance to society and the state, considering the senseless loss of lives, especially the innocent. Two, many states in the Union have radical laws that perpetuate this senseless loss of life; the most egregious being, enacting laws that allow for the unnecessary use of lethal force for self-defense in "events" that are safely avoidable.

Another argument may be presented as such: why guns? How about other arms? The constitution states *"arms"*—namely, swords, knives, perhaps, even javelins, stones, a bomb and so on? After all, people kill people; guns do not kill people. Nonetheless, this is an absurd cliché. Stray bullets are examples of guns killing people. If an individual intends to smite a person with a sword or other lethal means, that sword will not kill a person a mile away such as a stray bullet, or an off-target shot from a gun.

More so, ammunitions such as guns, facilitate murder, homicide, and terrorism. It is harder for a foreign or domestic terrorist to invade a public arena, execute and injure people massively with a knife, sword, stone, and so on. After the unfortunate death of one or two, capable ordinary citizens will most likely subdue an evil perpetrator of this sort.

• • •

15

Though, one might argue that explosive incendiary devices may do so; nevertheless, owning and keeping (and using) such are recognizably not guaranteed by the law as a "right." And by this logic, owning a military hardware such as an AR-15 is equally illogical as keeping and bearing grenades. We can extrapolate these from the fact that arms in 1791 are not the same as those in 2016.

Intra-Social Liberty: Privileges, Immunities, and Rights

Intra-social liberty and failed states

If "bleeding Kansas" with and without Osawatomie's John Brown[18], and Billy the Kid's Wild West[19] are independent nations, they will, by today's standards be designated as "failed states." South Chicago, South Boston and many neighborhoods in Washington, DC, and other American cities—in fact, the city at large, will be, by the criteria of failed states, fit into the many indices of an unstable society.

By not rigorously disarming their civilians, such municipalities have failed to appropriately monopolize the legitimate use of force—a crucial hallmark of a strong state and functional *contract*. These local governments have failed in their capacity to effectively monopolize force, use it justly, to establish order in the societies they govern. Too, they have largely been failed by the federal government, that is, the federal government's intervention.

The constitutionality of "the preamble" and its implications

Without the need to invoke much of its history, the legal doctrine of the years of Courts' opinions or jurists' philosophies, and existing assumptions predicated upon prevailing jurisprudence; the Second Amendment's deep drench in equivocation is almost dubious. However, with *prima facie* interpretation as it is meant to be, despite its equivocations, there can be a sense of moderation in its debate, rather than a radical view in a way subversive to the provision that is threatening to human life and limb in a free society.

Let's start with the very premise of the constitution of the United States. The preamble to the constitution itself is part of the constitution

---

[18] See the history of John Brown's "holy crusade" and deadly violence in Kansas against slavery

[19] See the history of the notorious Billy the Kid (in Lincoln County, New Mexico in the 1870s); an "outlaw" lifestyle that is *not* mythical, but truly characteristic of the Wild West.

as much as any article or section is. It is by far unreasonable to argue against the proposition of the legality and constitutionality of the preamble, despite the fact that it is not inserted into articles and sections. Many opinions by the High Courts are argued and justified by the "Founders' intent." Why not the constitution's preamble? —That is, the very declaration of its objective.

These intents might be sought in the Founders' personal public opinions in written form, or collective opinions such as the Federalist Papers, even the sacred Declaration of Independence. Not all these, however, are constitutional. Even if by séances, the Founders' can be consulted and their minds deciphered, whatever post 1788 "advice" they may offer is of no use, for it is not placed on paper and ratified. The Declaration of Independence, however, nobly sets what should be American ethical standards. And, it therefore, stands as America's moral compass.

The "order of priorities" of the constitution are based on the preamble
The preamble sets the purpose and the objective of the constitution in perspective as thus:

> *"We the People of the United States, in Order to form a more perfect Union, establish Justice, insure domestic Tranquility, provide for the common defence, promote the general Welfare, and secure the Blessings of Liberty to ourselves and our Posterity, do ordain and establish this Constitution for the United States of America."*

And with an appropriate interpretation of the Second Amendment, there appears no contradiction to this preamble. In this preamble, a number of things stand out: there is an order of priorities in the organization of the instruments that orchestrate the machinery of justice. In addition to that sociopolitical "scale of preference," it is the most viable principle of a functional state or society.

First, justice is ensured. Liberty deprived is justice denied. Second, "domestic tranquility" is affirmed. In a world of unchecked ammunition ownership and reckless legal and illegal use thereof, the object of tranquility is defeated. Regardless of the what the Framers imply by "domestic tranquility," such as civil unrest from sociopolitical chaos and so on—firearm violence, nonetheless, violates that ideal. Third, it is this kind of society—one with justice and tranquility—that is necessary for, and worth preservation by, a "Common defense" against outside infiltrators and aggressors against the state. Your right, my death: what's the point? In other words, security and harmony must arise first within the state. And, it is important to note that "common defense" *transcends* self-defense. More so, without "common defense," there will be chaos wherein there will be multiple factional lines of violence.

Furthermore, the doctrine of *non vita, non libertas* defines the "general Welfare" owed by the government to its people in two major ways. First, the government by its almost aloof attitude towards enforcing existing provisions, as will be seen later, is failing in guaranteeing that welfare. The rule of law: the binding social contract is betrayed.

Second, without life, there is no welfare; for such welfare is impossible when citizens deprive one another of the gift of life—that is, that which is endowed by their Creator. And in this, the government is also complicit in its unwillingness to regulate arms, both deadly and benign for some unscrupulous reasons which will be described down the line.

To reiterate an emphasized thesis of this work, "the Blessings of liberty" for ourselves, or any successive generation, cannot be secured if many lives remain in constant danger in the current status quo of America's notions and government's aloofness or seemingly ineffectiveness.

• • •

The threat of misinformed interpretation of the Second Amendment on intra-social liberty

Intra-social liberty is that which is endowed and guaranteed among a people bound by geopolitical, ethnic, race or religion ties. But more commonly, where a state is heterogeneous in peoples—of different creed or from "every walk of life"—the liberty of geopolitical bounds is fundamental.

Weapon proliferation and ownership are subject to regulation under the provisions of the Second Amendment, and this will be espoused in details in this work.

The "one-way" and non-dichotomous view of the Second Amendment is a recipe for societal conflicts, lack of tranquility—sometimes in a discriminatory way since some societies within the United States suffer mortal unrests than others. This equals backwardness in human advances toward a more sophisticated and enlightened civilization.

In a dichotomous view[20], the Second Amendment, as will be discussed more elaborately, has "regulation" and "infringement" elements. The government's hesitance to capitalize upon this, often for political reasons, can lead to "out-of-hands" problems.

Furthermore, it objectively deviates from the political clouded "prefatory" and "operative" clauses the SCOTUS attempted to squeeze into the provision—that is, the Second Amendment—in its *Heller v. DC* ruling opinion.

A dichotomous view of the Second Amendment: regulation

President George Washington, in putting down the Whiskey Rebellion[21], demonstrated how the "regulation" element is of severe importance.

---

[20] Independently formulated without the influence of the SCOTUS's decision syllabus.

[21] In 1791 a tax on whiskey was proposed by then treasury secretary Alexander Hamilton under the first presidential Administration—that of President George Washington. The tax

The militia of the Pennsylvania rebels was not "well regulated," or, regulated at all—not recognized by the government—as the Second Amendment provision imposes:

> *A well regulated Militia, being necessary to the security of a free State, the right of the people to keep and bear Arms, shall not be infringed.*

Therefore, the militia rebelling against the federal government over taxation, is not a legitimate militia, not being "well-regulated." It poses a threat of anarchy to society. Many instances of this are not uncommon today, and these unregulated militias, are only taken seriously after a conspiracy to perpetuate crime or after perpetuation of an egregious crime.

But if a militia is to be "well regulated," can it regulate itself? Considering the multiple factions of organized militia? Unlikely. Regulation thus falls under the federal law enforcement mechanisms.

Antebellum "wars" of the so-called "bleeding Kansas" are older instances. There was also, the prohibition era "bleeding Chicago." And even now in the twenty-first century, Chicago, as well as many urban and rural areas are still bleeding profusely.

---

was instituted to pay the national debt incurred by the American Revolution. After noncompliance and organized militia armed rebellion in some Pennsylvania counties, Washington personally militarily led the army to quell the rebellion.

At all points in history, since the *establishment* of the United States as a nation, it is only in times of infamy has the government turned a blind eye to unregulated militia to act with impunity for nefarious political and "cultural" purposes by anti-progress cynics. The Ku Klux Klan intimidations, antebellum wars of Kansas, Jim Crow violence and so on are some examples.

Politicking chaos

When the government is drowned in confusion if regulation equals infringement, a crisis in Lincoln County emerges. And thus, you have a Billy the Kid running amuck in a society dominated by anarchy.

Regulation of armament does not imply infringement.

In the scenario of Lincoln County and many American "Lincoln Counties," Billy the Kid, his cohorts, and nemeses, were not militias, but vigilantes and thugs. If by depriving certain individuals of gun ownership by regulation, an assumption of infringement is made, the government is shying away from the legal ramifications of this sociopolitical subject and risks the positive functions of law and order. In fact, the job and responsibilities of law enforcement agents have become as dangerous as that of a soldier on the frontlines of a battlefield.

Politicking with social order imposes a risk of the stability of the society. It is an unscrupulous and dangerous game to play. Yet, many politicians in government fatuously play it.

There is much debate over the sanctity of life in the sociopolitical ethics of abortion in the United States today. This, like the understanding of the Second Amendment, is a rigidly polar political ideology and debate.

Unfortunately, and ironically, those who argue about the sanctity of prenatal life are unruffled by the sanctity of postpartum and postnatal[22] human life. Ubiquitous chaos, anarchism, social breakdown,

---

[22] Politicians cannot keep telling the public whenever there is a mass shooting that "s@#t happens" whereas when a baby is aborted, some advocate prosecuting the mother, the doctor who performs the procedure, and the closure of the clinic where this is performed. More so, it's always never the right time to have the discussion of gun regulation during the fallout of public shootings—these hacks only send "thoughts" and "prayers." All lives are equal; especial one that is not a prenatal; neonates, postnatal individuals, toddlers, children, adults—those with breath, reason, vitality, and are members of civil society. The

unwarranted waste of life in pockets of societies in the United States and even abroad, to them, is of little relevance.

INTER-SOCIAL LIBERTY
Uprising

In what manner shall the absolute right to bear arms be consequential to inter-social liberty? Undeniably a "regulated militia," rising to the defense of the state against the unjustified incursions of other states or other entities in the community of nations. As Jefferson penned, "When in the Course of human events, it becomes necessary for one people to dissolve the political bands which have connected them with another, and to assume among the powers of the earth, the separate and equal station…"

Should the preservation of that assumption of a "separate and equal station" justify wide and unchecked weapon ownership? No. In today's world, nations have standing armies; the most formidable one at the United States' disposal.

It is far inconceivable that the American military will face a defeat that necessitates guerilla warfare against a hostile invader. America maintains multiple layers of formidable security. Even so, the nation maintains a stockpile of ammunition that able bodies can access if the standing military proves to be vulnerable. Even for an embryo nation, still in its formative state, the colonies accessed a stockpile in Lexington.

Ridiculous advocacy

The advocacy of the "devotees" of a distorted view of the Second Amendment, is an argument predicated on the need for, among many, self-defense, hunting, "recreational pleasure," and a bulwark or deterrence against threats on intra-social liberty. While all these

closure or at least regulation of gun manufacturing companies should be equally advocated for by the same politicians.

● ● ●

arguments are valid, sophisticated weaponry is unnecessary to these ends, and thus, they must be regulated.

Also, if the self-defense argument is further expanded, with many carrying weapons freely in society, a new and an unstable "Wild West" will re-emerge, in fact, worse—if not now, then sooner or later. It's a backward trend in human civilization. The current ubiquitous and frequent murder and mass murder are largely not based on self-defense, but a sadistic utility of weapons.

In all, the majority of Americans are permitted to keep unlimited amount of weaponry—guns, specifically. And many other states permit the ownership of automatic and semi-automatic rifles. Only for the fear of an invading enemy army in an individual's home are such weapons necessary.

But even more absurd is the *thought* or advocacy of the right to such ownership for hunting. The hunting argument is the most bizarre. This is akin to going to war with beast and game.

Guns that kill and maim scarcely end up in the hands of the rural hunter; but the cities' domestic terrorists, the deranged, and gangsters. After all, Al Capone's men were not hunters.

Only the paranoid is wary of the checks and balances system of the government and law enforcement apparatus in the United States. And such paranoia, that the government may become tyrannical, and when it does, the people must revolt, is a panacea to anarchy. There are state militias—regulated. And in the worst scenario of the federal government's failure to abide by the rule of law, many of these militias can abandon their constitutional "bonds" to be subjected to the authority of the president of the United States; in other words, they can refuse federalization in this extreme unforeseen circumstance and mutiny.

Lastly, many "Anne Oakleys" are dissatisfied and are nervous that the government *will* infringe on their Second Amendment "rights" when there is any debate about gun regulation. This is an unintelligible contention. Even Anne Oakley doesn't need, nor do her acts justify, the need to own an M-16, AR-15 or an AK-47.

Those who invoke in the name of God and guns blaspheme His name; for God in Jesus Christ, is a pacifist in the context of radical "self-defense" desires, castle law, fetishes for guns and so on.[23] They bring politics into religion and make a mockery of Christianity. Any phrase where "God" and "guns" appears as a mantra is an insult to the Author of harmony and civility—the God of the New Testament.

The downsides: threats to inter-social liberty

While Jefferson's "tree"[24] is one which survival and existence are based on the "blood of tyrants and patriots," the dependence of such a "tree" on indiscriminate blood can make a nation vulnerable in many ways.

Internal violence and the lack of a coherently structured state open it to external threat: the state is weakened. "A house divided against itself cannot stand"[25] Abraham Lincoln, before his presidency, observed in a speech, and he noted too, that the United States (as of then, and still now) cannot be defeated from external threat.[26] Except, as he, Lincoln, posited, if the nation self-destructs.

We are not in a state of a Civil War; we are, however, on the edge of social instability and civil unrest, considering the frequency of firearm violent deaths. Besides gang violence (pervasive in inner cities and also not uncommon to the rural lands of America), there are mass shootings

---

[23] Matthew 5:38 – 42

[24] Jefferson, T (1787) Letter to William Stephen Smith. *The Papers of Thomas Jefferson, ed.* Julian P. Boyd, vol. 12, p. 356 (1955).

[25] House divided House Divided speech. Delivered by Abraham Lincoln in Springfield, Illinois on June 16, 1858

[26] Lincoln, A. (1838, January 27) The Perpetuation of Our Political Institutions: Address Before the Young Men's Lyceum of Springfield, Illinois

in malls, shops, schools, on the streets and so on where children and adults are often subject to victimization.

Non-state affiliated radicals prove to be more threatening, in fact; and, such evil zealots might as well take advantage of the country's misguided ideology of non-regulation.

Is there any justifiable reason of villainous actions of civilians turning weapons on military personnel—one of the state's instruments of securing peace at home and abroad, by their service—based in the United States? Yet, this is a repeated train of infamous events.[27]

Furthermore, unchecked gun ownership, having led to prevalent unjustifiable violence, and sometimes hate crimes, reduces the country to an element of international propaganda about the country's enduring form of government.

The nation is on a downward trend to be labeled a "failed state" if gun laws are not well balanced.

Who is secured? Even if secured at home, no one is secured in the mall, airport, campus, and a movie theater. And if all or majority of the populace will haul guns to these avenues to counter such threat to safety, the nation becomes a war zone.

It is noteworthy that all four assassinated American presidents were sent to their Maker by bullets. And few more took bullets, but their lives were spared. Many others were threatened, all these, almost invariably with a gun. Not only these, many lawmakers, officers and

---

[27] Shootings (that ranges from one to more than ten casualties) of military personnel have been perpetuated by both disturbed military members and civilians that threaten our civil system in recent history. March 24, 2014, Norfolk, VA; March 31, 2013, Quantico, VA; September 16, 2013, Washington, DC; November 5, 2009, Fort Hood, Texas; October 27, 1995, Fort Bragg, NC; June 20, 1994, Spokane, Washington—all these are among many incidences.

enforcers of law have all been injured or killed by a gun. Seldom is another type of weapon used.

If society plunges to the depth of the abyss of dysfunction, what will be the cost of its preservation?

Implications of "Life"

The foundation of the argument presented heretofore may be construed as divining an elephant's face from cloud formations, such as the "order of priority" in the constitution's preamble and the concept of *life* from the Declaration of independence. Nevertheless, whether these are the Framers', writer(s)'s or author(s)'s intent or not; it is a fitting paradigm to mount an argument of reason. And one way or the other, the fundamental objective of the arguments here, is to all the forms of reason, of justified ethos.

Deprivation of life is the *most* unjust deed. "No life, no liberty." For we cannot compute with figures to any degree, nor measure by scale, the grief that the ruckus over constitutional misconception has conferred on those whose loved ones have fallen victims to the loss of life and limb, those crippled, and those, who cannot count their loss having been deprived of life.

There may be a continual and raging debate in the society about abortion and the role of the government in its regulation. There is, however, one thing that is not negotiable: all postnatal lives (to include all living beings out of the womb) are sacred and must be preserved as the entities that maintain the liberty, and thus, all the rights conferred on an individual.

All lives are endowed with equal value to every member of society. Therefore, the civil society must vigorously pursue the consummation to cherish all lives and recognize their sanctity.

Some politicians within the realms of power and pundits seem to underestimate life *outside* the womb the way they advocate for gun ownership in the aftermath of outrageous firearm disasters and domestic terrorism. They in fact double down in the face of gun terrors.

Not that life *in* the womb is less important, but if these individuals will channel the same energy with which they proclaim to defend prenatal life to defending life egressed from the womb, then, gun manufacturers, gun shops, gun show event organizers will come under fire, as well as, yes, certain gun owners.

THE ENLIGHTENMENT, ARMS,
AND SOCIAL CONTRACT:
A BRIEF OVERVIEW

First, I do claim to be an authority on Enlightenment philosophy, however, this does not imply I am disqualified to briefly discuss it.

Second, hardliners on Second Amendment interpretation often use this *ideal* of the influence of Enlightenment thinkers to describe the Framer's intent on the provision. That is not the case here, rather than influencing their *intent*, here, the goal is exploring how their *thinking* might have been influenced.

Lastly, on the note of introduction to this discussion, in-depth examination of the philosophies of some of the Enlightenment thinkers is beyond the scope of this treatise: both those referenced and those omitted.

It should be noted that the Enlightenment thinkers described were *influences* on the Whigs who fashioned America. They were not the Enlightenment men on the Eastern end of the Atlantic who theorize a form of government. They were not the delegates that declared independence from Great Britain, convened to draft and sign the constitution and experiment with a new form of government; and, they do not have supreme authority on objectivity and morality.

These were Europeans under the realms of monarchy debating what a just and free society should look like. But a people separated from Europe by a great ocean, having been under the realms of European monarchy, are now sequestered from a non-consensual government, conferred with the blessing of self-determination.

Confronted with the task of creating a new nation—almost unprecedented in history—the builders must gather fitting information from the wisdom of history and writings of visionaries to forge a building manual.

The theme of social contract as constructed by the Enlightenment thinkers here is not the organization of states and governments. Rather, it is the role of the armament of the government by its law enforcement agents and its military, and the armament of its people, chiefly, the civilians.

Violence—its rhetoric and concept—in the cause of safety and liberty in a social construct is not an aberrant idea from what the Enlightenment men have propounded. The question is, to what end?

Thomas Jefferson, a philosopher in his own right wrote in a 1787 letter to William Stephen Smith, that "The tree of liberty must be refreshed from time to time with the blood of patriots and tyrants. It is its natural manure." [28, 29] Here, there is an implication of the clash of arms to sustain liberty, however, with such violence, directed at the government. For one can barely call a threatening neighbor or an encroaching civilian a "tyrant."

---

[28] Jefferson, T (1787) Letter to William Stephen Smith *The Papers of Thomas Jefferson, ed.* Julian P. Boyd, vol. 12, p. 356 (1955).

[29] This Jefferson well known quotation, referred here to sometimes as "Jefferson's tree," is alluded to several times because it is often erroneously invoked by extreme right Second Amendment advocates.

When the blood of tyrants and patriots mingle, most at times, only history can separate and identify them. More so, the American Civil War of 1860 – 1865 demonstrates that, though "a new nation, with a rebirth of liberty under God"[30] came into being, some militants had a different impression of the kind of liberty the manure of their blood will breed.

Jefferson's statement, however, to varying degree, is being misconstrued today. It noteworthy to point out that Jefferson's philosophy of government and the people's revolt as pointed out in the US Declaration of Independence, is that "...government long established should not be changed for *light* or *transient* reasons [emphasis added]." In other words, there is the need for moderation and patience in the democratic process.

That is, the tree of liberty can long survive without the nourishment of blood. And besides, the immeasurable pints of blood being shed today—in our society—is neither the blood of patriots nor tyrants.

Most of the Enlightenment thinkers, such as the great John Locke, David Hume, Jean-Jacques Rousseau, Algernon Sidney (early), and so on, that influenced American Whigs, that is, Revolutionaries, fundamentally opposed monarchy. European monarchy is substantiated by the so-called "divine right," that is, the power vested by the Almighty. Instead, these Enlightenment men were in favor of a civilian self-determined organized state: government by the consent of the governed.

Are arms necessary to these ends?

When the Americans and the French rid themselves of monarchy, they used organized militancy, though, the French revolution proved to be quite chaotic. But once a democratic government was installed in these two civil, modern, and "first world countries," the state soon quickly monopolized force (or violence, as Weber describes).

This is an evidence that the chaos of democracy is still subject to

---

[30] Gettysburg Address

the modern philosophies of individuals like Max Weber who posited that one of the attributes of a state is its ability to monopolize the use of force. This position is somewhat backed by Enlightenment thinkers such as the English philosopher Thomas Hobbes.

Hobbesian self-defense and armed violence within a social contract is not without the "supervision of law"—that is, a strong state agent. Steven Pinker, in evaluating Hobbes in his book, *The Better Angels of our Nature: Why Violence Has Declined,* simplified Hobbes' Leviathan[31]—his masterpiece on the historical trend of violence.

> The logic of the Leviathan can be summed up in a triangle. In every act of violence, there are three interested parties: the aggressor, the victim, and a bystander. Each has a motive for violence: the aggressor to prey upon the victim, the victim to retaliate, the bystander to minimize the collateral damage from their fight. Violence between the combatant may be called war; violence by the bystander may be called law. The Leviathan theory in a nutshell, is that the law is better than war.[32]

By "War," 'self-defense' is implied.

As mentioned before, the United States has modernized to have a strong law enforcement system, which has eliminated the necessity for American civilians to be at "war" when Hobbes wrote the Leviathan (1651). In fact, Hobbes went on to write, as Pinker noted, that "savage people in many places in America" are existing in a state of anarchy.

---

[31] Hobbes, T. (1651) Leviathan
[32] Pinker, S. (2011) The Better Angels of our Nature: Why Violence Has Declined [Pg. 33]

Well, regardless of what Hobbes meant by that, this is the 21st century America.

While Pinker's work is broad in addressing crime and violence zigzagging across time and history, the major thesis in this essay addresses gun proliferation, questionable ownership, and the consequent disregard for human life. America's policy in this regard is equally flawed and nebulous. More so, the ubiquitous and frequent mass shootings that seem to have been normalized in the United States in the 21st century is an absolute dishonor, considering the relative peace in its counterpart civilized nations, and this epoch in contrast with the barbaric ancient generations.

Statistics may present a dilemma; homicide has shown a downward trend since the last couple of decades or so. Therefore, mass shootings are masked by the façade of that statistic.

The fact is *safety*— of individuals and the public—constitutes one of the foundational principles upon which the United States is built as invoked in the Declaration of Independence. In this age, however, that fundamental value is gravely threatened.

A government, the Declaration argues, must be the one that will be "…most likely to effect… [individuals'] *Safety* and Happiness…" This guarantee and principle are thus threatened, when a citizen who has gone shopping in a mall or departmental store, might return in a body bag, along with other shoppers—not because of an offense they have perpetuated towards the shooter, but for unintelligible and tongue-tied reasons. This also applies to pupils whom their parents have sent to school and are looking forward to picking them up from school—alive; also, college campuses, airports, and more abominably, places of worship. As Americans, we are not safe—neither in a public sphere or private enclosures.

The fundamental ideals of democracy in a liberal society become questionable when the sacred and inalienable right to live is not a guarantee. And worse still, is that this status quo as it stands today in the United States, is the consequence of ineffective law enforcement, discrimination, inept governance, and the government's betrayal of social contract.

To paraphrase Jean-Jacques Rousseau, the agreement to enter into civil society is a social contract which binds individual in mutual preservation. In doing so, people sacrifice the physical freedom of being able to do *whatever* they please; and, only under such an arrangement, can we become fully human—that is, rational and moral humans.

There is a tendency to exaggerate self-defense from other people who are in civil society and the government itself. This leads to two things: devaluation of life and anarchy.

However, even Thomas Hobbes, in arguing for social contract, contends that it requires the rule of absolute sovereign—one which one in *modern* times can be interpreted as strong law enforcement. He contends that "the brute situation of the state of nature ("the war of all against all") could only be avoided by strong, undivided government."

This is consistent with "a well regulated militia..." the "prefatory clause," as interpreted by SCOTUS in *DC v Heller*" or the regulation clause of the Second Amendment. It will be misleading to attribute that to Hobbes, but this section of this treatise, only explores how the Enlightenment individuals reasoned.

It is important to point out that this work, the Leviathan, was composed during the English Civil war of 1642–1651. And, the American Revolutionaries, in their case, were constitutionally constructing the framework of a new nation, not engaged in a civil war.

Even during the instability of the American Civil War, it was the government's fervent move to monopolize force and quench insurrection of the rebels, that restored a broken country and the rule of law. The American South's revolt was counter-democratic.

When a possible righteous revolution 2.0 might happen, is paranoia, because the Founders by the genius of the flawed constitution they left, added countermeasures to it to make it foolproof for the Republic. Power is divided into branches of government, and military power, though still under the country's commander-in-chief, is distributed down to the states, too; with states maintaining a relatively minimal sovereignty. Therefore, in a moral contest, in this Republic, the likelihood is that the voices of reason will prevail.

So, shall we consider the following: what is social contract according to Enlightenment philosophers? And what is the role of civilian armament in it? How is the rule of law assessed by ancient thinkers, and more importantly, common sense? How should the government be kept in check by the governed in terms of arms? Because it is under this pretext that the nation is at homicidal war with itself.

While Rousseau believes that only through the agreement with which individuals enter a civil society that binds people into a community that exists for mutual preservation, he believes people sacrifice the physical freedom of being able to do whatever they please, but they gain in return the civil freedom of being able to think and act rationally and morally.

This does not imply that individuals are to give up their lives in pacifism and passivity. The implication is that the primitive cruelty of devaluation of life is (or should be) abolished in a civilized society.

David Hume presents an *Original Contract*[33].

The point of all these "contracts" is for the collective civil existence of humans, not as cannibalistic chimpanzees.

"The conditions under which [*all*][34] are willing to submit, were either expressed, or so obvious, that it might well esteemed superfluous to express them. If thus, then, be meant by the *original contract*, cannot be denied, that all government is, at first founded on contract..." Hume posited. However, he neither stops nor begins here. As a thought

---

[33] Hume, D. (1748) "Of the Original Contract"
[34] Emphasis added

• • •

35

experiment, he takes his reader on an adventure to antiquity "when we can trace government to its first origin to the woods and deserts." Nevertheless, even these primitive societies, to form a functional community "...abandon their native liberty, and receive law equal and companion..." This is the very beginning of the *original contract*.

Therefore, the rule of law is guaranteed under such a contract.

The most constructive influence of the Enlightenment philosophers on the Founders is particularly the *form of government* fitting for a free people. And the chief architect among these thinkers is John Locke. To capitalize on that, in terms of the American form of government, even the Declaration of Independence is often misinterpreted by some so-called "patriots" today.

For instance, as noted in the text "...That whenever any Form of Government becomes destructive of these ends, it is the Right of the People to alter or to abolish it, and to institute new Government, laying its foundation on such principles and organizing its powers in such form, as to them shall seem most likely to effect their Safety and Happiness." That is, say the presidential system of government is no longer effective; we can alter it for a parliamentary one. Or, a unicameral Congress can be adopted, with the lower or upper house getting the ax. It takes "absolute despotism" to overthrow a government. This is yet to materialize and is unlikely to.

However, there is something else very notable in the Declaration: that is one with a form of government that "...guarantees the *safety* and happiness" of its people. Shootouts and massive homicides are anathema to that creed, and the government's inaction defies it.

These aforementioned influences of no doubt left a lingering *tradition* transcribed from their thoughts, in which *individual* rights to bear and keep arms was neither criminalized nor constitutionalized by Founders. However, some states legalized the tradition by legislative or constitutional measures, and others made it a *de facto* law by not criminalizing the tradition.

This armament and self-defense tradition has been cemented into the American tradition as European settlers flood into the continent and saw the need to tame, subjugate and conquer it for their happiness, safety, and security. Taming, as to tame the wilderness—the expanse of America and its wildlife; subjugate, as to put indentured humans in chattel slavery at bay and deter rebellion. Lastly, conquer, as to conquer the indigenous inhabitants of the land: I came, I saw, I conquered. By arms.

As will be reiterated in observing John Locke, Enlightenment philosophers indeed embraced self-defense, as part of an organized civil society, but not to the extent it has been taken in many cases in the United States.[35] "Castle Laws" are a radical example of these.[36] More so, they also proposed the necessity of revolution from a tyrannical government, however, cautiously: a strong government submitted to the rule of law is fundamental to a society where anarchy must be avoided. As Hume argued, it is an arrangement as this that makes members of society civil. As Jean-Jacques Rousseau, pointed out:

---

[35] On November 14, 2007, in Pasadena, Texas, Jon Horn, a native of Houston, shot and killed two African-American buglers intruding on his neighbor's home. After a call to the 911 dispatch, with a clear instruction not to interfere, he took action regardless. He was cleared from the homicides because of the State's "castle law."

Lave, T. R. (2013, September 4). Shoot to Kill: A Critical Look at Stand Your Ground Laws. Retrieved August 5, 2016

[36] Lindgren, J. (2007, February 27). The Lockean right of self-defense—and stand-your-ground laws. Retrieved August 05, 2016, from https://www.washingtonpost.com/news/volokh-conspiracy/wp/2014/02/27/the-lockean-right-of-self-defense-and-stand-your-ground-laws/

• • •

> The passage from the state of nature to the civil state produces a very remarkable change in man, by substituting justice for instinct in his conduct, and giving his actions the morality they had formerly lacked. Then only, when the voice of duty takes the place of physical impulses and right of appetite, does man, who so far had considered only himself, find that he is forced to act on different principles, and to consult his reason before listening to his inclinations...[37, 38]

The vote is still an arsenal of civilian power in an authentic democratic state like the United States. Overwhelming armament and a militarized population are counterintuitive to the ideals of a stably established government: a form of government that Locke and Hume are advocating for.

Whatever these philosophers propose on self-defense, and to what extent, their doctrines are almost invariably counterbalanced by the need of peace in human co-existence in a civilized society. And more so, the need of strong government as a mediator of that peace.

Lockean view of self-defense is more radical, yet, Locke's philosophy points to a government's role in mediating crises that will mitigate the otherwise use of excessive force by individuals in a civil society.

Yet, John Locke understood that with a government in place, the chaos of "war" as he puts it, will be minimized under the maxims of self-defense. If Locke's coat or horse were stolen, he justifies killing the aggressor: the aggressor having declared a "war" against him.

---

[37] Rousseau, J (1762). The Social Contract or the Principles of Political Rights [Pg. 14]. Translated by G.D.H. Cole

[38] It is worth noting that all the philosophers here differ significantly on other subjects and approached this very subject from different lens of the same prism.

However, if he can appeal to an arbitrator—a judiciary in government, then that changes the ethics. As he puts it:

> ...[I]n the state of nature, where no such appeal is, as in the state of nature, for want of positive laws, and judges with authority to appeal to, the state of war once begun, continues, with a right to the innocent party to destroy the other whenever he can, until the aggressor offers peace, and desires reconciliation on such terms as may repair any wrongs he has already done, and secure the innocent for the future. . .[39]

Since the influence of this famous physician/philosopher—that is, John Locke—on the framers of this nation was so profound, it seems that they understood that government serves an equally profound role in society as an arbitrator. And thus, making government extremely significant; reducing the violence that results from the right of an individual's self-defense to a "common Judge."

Even if the United States constitution guarantees an individual's right to bear arms, such as the states' analogues as will be described further, Jefferson was clever enough to know that laws can carry an expiration date. As Jefferson wrote:

> I think moderate imperfections had better be borne with; because, when once known, we accommodate ourselves to them, and find practical means of correcting their ill effects. But I know also, that laws and institutions must go hand in hand with the progress of the human mind. As that becomes more developed,

---

[39] Locke, J. (1690). Second Treatise on Government [Chapter 3 #20]. His expression of "war" means violence.

> more enlightened, as new discoveries are made, new
> truths disclosed, and manners and opinions change
> with the change of circumstances, institutions must
> advance also, and keep pace with the times. We might
> as well require a man to wear still the coat which fitted
> him when a boy, as civilized society to remain ever
> under the regimen of their barbarous ancestors.[40]

Society becomes more complex with time, with new assumptions needing a new set of laws, or a review of the old ones, within the confines of liberal and democratic principles.

Although we take his words with Apostolic or prophetic authority, Locke is another individual—one revered thinker. His treatises were completed in 1689. Times, nevertheless, have changed. This is neither the Renaissance nor Enlightenment. This is a new age, which posterity will christen, such as we have described the ages before us, such as the Medieval, Renaissance, and Enlightenment and so on.

And while he, Locke, might state without equivocation that an act of aggression such as robbery justifies lethal defense, he, collectively with other Enlightenment philosophers agreed that, by individuals in a society entering a contract, they sacrifice some of their rights to be governed. This implies that the government is an arbiter in all criminal cases. And a person is restricted from taking laws into his own hands most especially when his life is not faced with a mortal threat from another. And as long as the government doesn't fail that obligation, citizens are subjected to the law.

Besides, the United States is competent in law enforcement to

---

[40] Jefferson, T (1816, July 12) Letter to H. Tompkinson (also Samuel Kercheval). Jefferson's correspondence c. 1816: some 27 years after the constitution went into effect and becomes operational

guarantee the safety and security of its citizens, in this age. Where it fails is the security and guarantee of the lives that fall victim to the proliferation of weaponry. Among many examples, children in school cannot "wage war" on an adult aggressor with an assault rifle.

More so, it is noteworthy to point out that the radical notions of violence of an *individual's* self-defense and, too, vigilante-style "self-defense" became a *tradition* in the United States as the embryo state adopted, for instance, the form of government set forth by Locke and others. Many jurisdictions within the society constitutionalized or legislated it. The US Bill of Rights, however, enumerated "A well regulate Militia…"

Therefore, the United States did not constitutionalize it, but it continued to be a celebrated tradition of its free society. Nevertheless, moderation has been tossed out of this tradition of possessing weaponry. Not only recently, but from the days of territorial wildness, say, the colonial days to the in the days of raging Wild West and the age of dueling, that Hobbes might have referred to as when "savage people in many places in America" are existing in a state of anarchy.

GLADIUS ET LIBERTAS
(SWORD AND LIBERTY)

The bold credo of the State of New Hampshire is *"Live free or die."* And this is a "mellifluent" rhetoric of the free spirit of the Republic: that citizens shall not be subjugated. And while human government is truly predisposed to despotism, it is not the character of the social contract of modern society—especially, Western democracies today.

Considering this, if "live free or die" were applied nationally, many *are* dying in a free society while others wield the sword, in many cases, recklessly and unnecessarily.

The cries of self-defense, hunting, and recreation is amazingly why many cling to the idea of unrestricted ownership of firearms.

Besides, there are business interests that stand to gain from the unrestrained proliferation, and, of citizens acquiring their manufactured products. Therefore, they hide behind a banner of these powerful interests' malevolent capability to sway and intimidate government officials and political hacks. Too, they are able to influence national dialogue to their ulterior advantage.

Symbolism of Sandy Hook

We are in an age of Sandy Hook.

Children martyred by bullets piercing their frail flesh, now soaring in frequency and in expanding ubiquity, are now characteristic of the American society. An unfortunate unsurprising tale of a sophisticated nation among the family of industrialized and "first world" nations. It is an abysmal shame. A tale of savagery.

This is a nation that is supposed to have a literate population—men and women of reason; a nation that prides itself in exceptionalism in the ideal of people living freely. Is this the idea of the "home of the brave": existing in the jungle of flying bullets and being proud of it?

People die by the thousands every day in the inner cities, city outskirts, suburbia, towns, and hamlets of the nation without the due traction of national media. It is the norm of our violent culture, which makes the United States consistently rank as one of the most dangerous places to live in the world for the "cause" of liberty mortally abused. Law enforcement agencies only present periodically statistics, and, this seldom gain the attention of American journalists.

However, unfortunate events, savagery ones such as killings of the defenseless in Columbine, West Nickel Mines, and Sandy Hook in a year dominated by mass murder, are always ever before us. Hadiya Pendleton, killed by a stray bullet, was a martyr of a society that has undermined the value of life. Mass massacres such as the ones that occurred at Virginia Tech, Tucson, and Aurora make the United States seem like a country with guerilla war being waged to terrorize the government and the populace.

Events like these demonstrate that one of the most potent terror threats to the society is firearms, being as common as not too rare household appliances. What is the probability that a child, when he departs from school in the morning, will return home in the afternoon? And also, that a young romantic couple will return from a movie theater? Or that a teenager in a shopping mall won't be taken out in a body bag?

These are just a few areas where lunatics and deranged zealots, and in some cases, sane individuals with ulterior motives lurk as predators to harm for no reason than infamy. It is fair to say without equivocation, that easy access to firearms facilitates these abhorrent incidences.

AMERICAN YOUTHS AND VIOLENT DEATH

Nothing is more traumatic to a generation of a country than a lethal threat to the security of adolescents as it is for juveniles, too. Eight-year-olds undergo drills in school just like the White House staff to prepare for terrorism—in their case, most likely, domestic terrorism.

Notwithstanding, innocent teenagers being gunned down on American streets, both in inner cities and "outer cities"—appropriately put, city outskirts— is an indication of the loss of the nation's moral compass especially when nothing is being done about it. Surely, there is a loss of moral compass when a vigilante like George Zimmerman can be acquitted for killing a seventeen-year-old for strolling the street based on a state's abhorrent Castle Law.

Parents of minority children—of Americans of African Ancestry and Hispanics—panic and live in constant fear of the wellbeing of their teenage boys. This is a daily anxiety. Not just their wellbeing, but also their longevity, life expectancy, threatened not only by the hands of bandits with legal and illegal weapons but chiefly and unfortunately, law enforcement, particularly the police.

The pathos of this status quo of the psychological injury on the national consciousness of American young people and their parents is agonizing. This is the country we live in, and, this is where "the Second Amendment" has left us.

Hadiya Pendleton & Trayvon Martin

Many teenage Americans of all races and religions are victims of firearms violence and death. However, the case of Hadiya Pendleton and Trayvon Martin brought the ethos of the slaughtering of American youth to public spectacle. This publicity, protest, and plea to government officials achieved nothing.

Pendleton, 15, is an honor student and had participated in her marching band during the inaugural festivities of the 44th president of the United States. She will be shot a few days afterward. Her death, as with many deaths, raises a lot of questions such that, it will take volumes to detail.

According to a *Time* report by Madison Gray dated January 30, 2013, Senator Dick Durbin, (D) IL, raised the issue during the congressional hearing on gun violence. It is great that he raised the issue, but the deeper content of his comments is what invoked a somber thought: "Just a matter of days after the happiest day of her life, she's gone" Durbin said referencing her death after her participation in the inaugural parade for President Obama. He, Durbin, continued, maintaining that "We have guns everywhere and some believe the solution to this is more guns. I disagree."

First, the youth was robbed of her life and therefore, her liberty for the pursuit of her happiness. Pendleton, from reports, is a vibrant girl full of life. An honor student attending an elite prep school, she is also a majorette in her school's marching band that has performed in several inaugurations.

Having been *endowed* by life by her Creator, she is in the pursuit of happiness. According to a report by Karen McVeigh on Thursday, January 31, 2013, in *The Guardian*, the youth's father, Nathaniel Pendleton, mentioned the murderer(s) had extinguished the "light of my life." Continuing, "Look at yourself, just know that you took a bright person, an innocent person, a nonviolent person." This is the anguish of a procreator.

More importantly, according to the same report, she had dreams of attending the nation's prestigious Northwestern University (not far from home), becoming a pharmacist, a journalist, and perhaps a lawyer. Is it inconceivable to be all of these? You may ask someone like Dr. Sanjay Gupta, the neurosurgeon, journalist, and writer. Besides, many tertiary intuitions now offer dual professional degrees. As to what Pendleton could have achieve, we'll never know.

Furthermore, according to Gray's report, Chicago police officer and Pendleton's godfather Damon Stewart volunteered that "that the teen was always making big plans." Big plans in the pursuit of happiness—big plans for her future.

"She was working on some sort of exchange program, where she was going to go to school in Paris," her godfather said. "She was a great student." But her pursuit of happiness was ended with an assassin's bullet, having done absolutely nothing wrong remotely justifiable for such a punishment: violent death.

Because of the guns on the streets of America, she did not get to bargain her right to live. She could not bargain for all the potentials her fighting spirit and thriving intellect can offer: the society, having demolished the room she had to blossom, and also deprived her of her God-given liberty. She's young, she's innocent, she's slain. And all these burdens, occurring in 21st century America

On the other hand, as the usual argument goes: Pendleton wasn't killed by a gun. She was killed by someone else—someone with a misplaced morale. Perhaps. But a knife or a rock hauled at her at that distance is far less likely to have killed her. Further, the proliferation of weapons and the illegal smuggling of weaponry into municipalities with tougher regulation laws help place these weapons in the wrong hands. This was the president's contention as he pushed back NRA's assertions according to *The Guardian* report by McVeigh.

The NRA is yet unmolested. Their mantra still remains guns and more guns: gun is the cure for gun violence. Someone ought to be outraged to a noticeable degree, and to that degree, that will shed a bright light on this barbarism and effect change.

If you are a mother and your teenage child—male or female—is being bullied, you will feel in the depths of maternity, the pain of your child being tormented. Seldom can any parent or guardian escape the feeling of some powerlessness to have defended an injury inflicted upon their child and agonize over shielding their child from further suffering.

But what if a bullet were to pierce the body of a parent's child? And the next time they get to see their child is in a morgue? Pendleton, a child who has no arrest records and had never been a troublesome youth got caught in a crossfire of urban violence. How about one that is slain—even against the advice of law enforcement call center after his murderer called an emergency line to report a suspicious youth?

Trayvon Martin, 17, was murdered on February 26, 2012, by a neighborhood vigilante, George Zimmerman. Martin was unarmed, and the details of the provocation that led to his death is a matter of national controversy.

The case of Martin taints America making it stand out as an exception in the developed world with the malignant issue of deadly violence on young people and the impotency or discrimination of the justice system.

Note that Martin was not assaulted in a mass shooting as unfortunate of many juveniles. Nor was he victimized by police brutality as it's been ubiquitous in postbellum America, Jim Crow America up to Barack Obama's America. He was gunned down under the presumption that he represents a threat—a perceived threat predicated upon his race and attire.

This is an abysmal assault on the national consciousness of American youth and, to put it more charitably, an embarrassment to the country. Totalitarian regimes like Russia's Vladimir Putin, as a propaganda, will point to these events as normalized chaos, and the impossibility of perfect justice: "as it is in Russia, so it is in the United States." If we've reached the epoch where minors consider themselves vulnerable species in American juggle, we are in a dangerous fix.

Too, Martin, unlike Pendleton, was not caught in a crossfire of gang violence. It is noteworthy to point to this fact. His slaying, like others like him, is unfortunately and infamously unique.

More so, as it will be discussed in the epilogue, the youthful 22-year old Christina Grimme, a music rising star was shot Saturday, June 10, 2016, by a disturbed man who was able to smuggle in two firearms to an Orlando concert. Her cold-blooded untimely death can, and should be blamed squarely and fairly on American terrible gun laws. Her shooter should by no means have had the rights to bear or keep arms.

The Bill of Rights:
Dissecting the Second Amendment
and its Elusive Intent

On December 15, 1791, after ratification, the constitution was amended with provisions grouped into ten enumerations. These amendments are contained within what is referred to as the Bill of Rights—ten from the several proposed: voted in both chambers of Congress and ratified by the states. This was accomplished after some tumultuous public political discourse, the controversy surrounding the amendments being, undocumented rights might be abridged.

However, after over two centuries of American jurisprudence, these issues are still subject to intense scrutiny; unfortunately, interpreted with the rigid lens of partisanship and ideology. There have been several precedencies—majority and minority opinions from the United States Supreme Court, an encyclopedia in law libraries dedicated to the analyses of *one* of these Bill of Right provisions in the shortest constitution written in the English language.

Most importantly, considering the scope of this subject regarding constant explosions of "war zones" inside the United States, a lifetime of study can be embarked upon on the controversy of the Second Amendment:

> A well regulated Militia, being necessary to the security of a free State, the right of the people to keep and bear arms shall not be infringed.

This is the most contentious law, probably in any jurisdiction. Short, concise, but annoyingly nebulous. Did the Founders deliberately frame it as such? The common assumption and position are, all subject to the jurisdiction of the statute have the indisputable and unrestrained right to keep and bear arms. And subtly, the three arms of the federal government have swayed the law with the very *weak* exemption of felons and the stigmatized mentally ill in *some* cases.

TWO CLAUSES

Burying the prism of ideology, which deflects objectivity away from accurate perception several degrees away, this amendment *should* be 'interpreted' in similitude to the Freedom of Religion provision of the First Amendment. Both the so-called right and left of the political spectrum, practicing and academic constitutional lawyers have not evaluated the Second Amendment this way—that is, in any significant sense.

The Freedom of Religion provision of First Amendment is naturally divided into two clauses, namely "establishment" and "prohibition" clauses, both invariably mutually inclusive. Therefore, if "Congress shall make no law respecting an establishment of religion" it must also make no law "prohibiting the free exercise thereof."

In fact, neither the "Freedom of speech" clause, nor the restraints of states on religion establishment and prohibition as instituted by the First and reinforced by the Fourteenth Amendment, are narrowly interpreted and judicially applied like the Second. So, why should the Second Amendment be more sacrosanct than the First—the statue protecting the very fundamental Civil Rights of individuals in our society?

The infringement and regulation clauses

Although the Second Amendment can hardly be simplified, it can, within all measures of reason, be interpreted in the fashion of the "establishment" and "prohibition" clauses. This way, the Second Amendment can be split into two: the "regulation" clause (or phrase) and the "infringement" clause. Looking at it this way, while "the right of the people to keep and bear arms, *shall* not be *infringed*" it *must* also be *regulated*, in fact, "well regulated."

Thus, we can interpret the law on the basis of the "regulation" and the "infringement" 'clauses.' One, "A well regulated Militia, being necessary to the security of a free State," the *regulation*, and two, "the right of the people to keep and bear arms shall not be infringed," *the infringement* clause.

Why, nonetheless, did the 'rectifiers' of this Amendment opened it with the preamble: "A well regulated Militia"? This opens a host of questions that any ten randomly chosen Americans can seldom provide the same answer to. And this reveals the complexity of the debate in a population of about 320 million people with a significant fraction of politically active and sharply polarized persons.

There are few regulation clauses in the constitution

Besides the "well *regulated* militia," there is another constitutional regulation provision, which without equivocation of jurists and law enforcers, is executed as stipulated.

Article I, Section 8, Clause 3, is a well-known and thoroughly kept regulation clause. And that is "the commerce regulation clause." Like a "Well regulated militia being necessary for the security of a free state," the constitution stipulates that "Congress shall have power to regulate Commerce with foreign Nations, and among the several states…" Now, a militia—or a person's right to bear and keep arms—that must be "well regulated" *cannot* regulate itself. Only the state can institute statutes of regulation even if the constitution does not explicitly stipulate that Congress should be the entity to regulate it.

"ELEMENTS" OF THE SECOND AMENDMENT
What is a militia?
The one or more of the men who drafted the constitution in 1787 might have possessed John Marchant's 18th Century dictionary. And thus, the grammar of the elite must have been polished by it. Published in 1760 in London, the volume also co-authored by D. Bellamy and Gordon, is said to be "a new complete English dictionary…Wherein difficult words and technical terms in all faculties and professions are fully explained…"

Marchant's dictionary, published twenty-seven years before the drafting of the constitution and thirty-one years before the ratification of the Bill of Rights, defines 'militia' as thus:

> In general, denotes the body of soldiers, or those who make the profession of arms. But in a more restrained sense, it denotes the trained bands of a town or country, who arm them themselves upon a short warning, for their defense.

So, according to this definition, what is a *militia*?
1.	It includes a body of soldiers.
2.	It describes those who make a profession of arms, such as, non-traditional soldiers—contracted soldiers etcetera.
3.	It also connotes individuals who are "trained bands," "restrained," and are, therefore, combatants for the defense of their country and/or community. This definition equally

includes "standby"—reserves—trained combatants to be conscripted in wartime.

4. In all of these cases, a militia is a "band" or "body" of individuals—they are in the *profession* of arms and are *trained*. This, to a constructive or destructive—though, this definition implies only the constructive—ends.

The elements of this definition were prominent during the Revolutionary War. Among the fighting force, there were the "regulars" the "colonies' militia" and "other forms of militia" that are quickly assembled, organized, trained and channeled into the battlefield.

Therefore, during the Revolutionary War, a militia is a fighting force not part of the "official" central government's "standing army." Few distinct types of militia existed then, the militia which is a *colony's* official military which morphed into the modern-day national guard of each state in the Union. Also, the militia that comprised of yeomen, rags, and riches; volunteered men fighting alongside military officers. And, despite their autonomous skirmishes, they were largely regulated.

The militia uprising[41] during the presidency of George Washington known as the Whisky Rebellion was put down by federal force to the dismay of some of the president's compatriots. This rebelling militia was illegitimate, not being "well regulated"—that is, endorsed by the government. Their illicit agenda had to be crushed by the government: the component of the state that should monopolize force. So, what is that "militia" that must be well regulated?

To better resolve the ambiguity, the etymology and the history of the usage of the word "militia" needs to be considered. According to Merriam-Webster, the word is a Latin derivative of military service *milit-, miles*. And the first known usage was known to be in 1625.

---

[41] See reference 21

Even today, all the definitions provided, imply a "group" or part of it—consistent with Marchant's definition—such as (Merriam-Webster's definition): (1A) "a part of the organized armed forces of a country liable to call only in emergency." Also, (1B) "a body of citizens organized for military service." It offers a second definition: "the whole body of able-bodied male citizens declared by law as being subject to call to military service." And finally, a generalized definition is "a *group of people* who are *not part of the armed forces* of a country but are *trained like soldiers*. [emphasis added]"

The key point: a person or an individual *is not* a militia. And an individual who has joined or who have been conscripted into a militia is *well trained* in the use of arms. And in a civil society, common sense dictates that all militias as defined here will be subject to the government's or the people's authority, especially in a democracy.

Lastly, the Framers', being cognizant of the English language as used and spoken properly in their times as the etymology and previous definition suggested, will be reckless to sign an amendment so erroneous if the militia in question is a *person* or American civilians in general. As Justice Stevens noted in the *Heller* case,

> "the Amendment is most naturally read to secure
> to the people a right to use and possess arms in
> conjunction with service in a well-regulated militia"

What is a "free state"?

The Amendment further states that this "militia", that is being well regulated, is "…necessary for the security of a free State…" It is not uncommon to capitalize all nouns as standard written English language in the 18th century. So, what free state? If we shall suppose that the "people" in the Amendment refers literally to the population, then, *five* possible "states" can be construed.

That is, if the "militia" in question, is not another structured group of *people*, for instance, those that represented the nation in Philadelphia during the Constitutional Convention in 1787 and styled themselves as "we the people" in the preamble to the constitution. Obviously, this phrase does not constitute *all* the people in the United States at the time; similarly, we can consider the *people's* army, navy, etcetera, to be those in uniform posited for the first line of the defense of the American people.

A free state can be evaluated as thus:

1. First, a "state" such as the nation-state of America can be implied; in this case, when confronted by an external threat to its freedom and sovereignty, then this "well regulated Militia" can grab their arms and rush to its defense.

2. Second, is still the nation-state of America; when a government within resorts to despotism, then, this "militia" heeds the call to arms and overthrow such government. Just as Thomas Jefferson noted, that "The tree of liberty must be refreshed from time to time with the blood of patriots and tyrants..."[42] However, constant conflict by firearms as a means of opposition to the government in a democracy creates a failed state. A true democracy offers—especially a democracy with a genuine integrity of enfranchisement—many other platforms as an alternative to violence.

3. The next possible "state" is a state in the Union, so that, when any political device tends to destroy the republican government of the nation, then this "militia"—that is the militia of a state—can secure the free state, i.e., *that* State in the Union.

4. Also, a "state" one could imagine, is the sociopolitical *condition* of individuals in the nation-state.

---

[42] See reference 28

• • •

5. Lastly, a type of state which carries much equivocation is the general *status quo*. The integrity of liberty in the state-of-affairs: freedom from societal chaos.

The Second Amendment: What is "arms"?

The last question, and the most important, is what constitute "arms." A gun is an arm, but an arm is *not* necessarily a gun. As judicial activists on the Courts' bench often argue, the law must keep up with time, as time must keep up with the law; even Jefferson, whose visionary "tree" will only be kept blossoming when occasionally watered by the blood of tyrants and patriots, envisioned the same.[43] And while the ethics of judicial activism is questionable, the concept is laudable in some cases. "I am certainly not an advocate for frequent and untried changes in laws and constitutions." Jefferson contended in his missive. He had wrestled with the idea of the constancy in the forms of law that govern a society and such as the society is accustomed to.

However, he went on to set out a maxim that should shape the *thinking* of lawmakers and jurists:

> I think moderate imperfections had better be borne with; because, when once known, we accommodate ourselves to them, and find practical means of correcting their ill effects. But I know also, that laws and institutions must go hand in hand with the progress of the human mind. As that becomes more developed, more enlightened, as new discoveries are made, new truths disclosed, and manners and opinions change with the change of circumstances, institutions must advance also, and keep pace with the times. We might as well require a man to wear still the

---

[43] Ibid

coat which fitted him when a boy, as civilized society
to remain ever under the regimen of their barbarous
ancestors.[44]

We may not go that far as calling our ancestors "barbarous."
But for instance, in the 1770s a gun is a "simple" pistol or musket,
and a bayonet. Today, a gun could be anything like a Bushmaster, a
sophisticated pistol or handgun, or automatic rifles such as M-16 or
AK-47 and complicated ones meant to destroy a battalion at whim.

What else are *arms*? That is, arms an individual is entitled to keep
and bear? Could it be a tank, nuclear arsenal, a Tomahawk missile,
warheads, bombs, or private standing army and a fleet of naval ships?

Whereas, perhaps in the 18th century it may not be farfetched for
someone to be in the possession of artillery on his farm. Today can a
person have an Abrams tank in his driveway? Or today's artillery that
can deliver much potent and devastating ordinance at disposal? In as
much as such *arms* can be regulated, thus implying that *some arms* can
be regulated, then, all *arms* can and should be regulated.

It, therefore, seems a good way to clear the controversy is to call a
constitutional convention or initiate a constitutional amendment in the
barely living Congress. The so-called red, blue, and purple states will
have a hard time concurring to this. If this happens, as it should be, *we*
should change the current language of the Second Amendment, and
replace it with one that is unequivocal in implication. The Amendment
as it is today is too vague for a consensus in interpretation and
application.

Amending the Amendment?
The American constitution is oldest and continuously legal document in
effect in the world (the Magna Carta, aside). This is noble. But as sacred

---

[44] See reference 40

as that nobility is, the practicability of many of the document's statutes, in application and relevance to a time that has shifted so significantly from the eighteenth century, is lacking. The Third Amendment might as well be a joking stock to millennials.

In a sense, the US Constitution that came out of the 1787 convention, ratified in 1788 and adopted in 1789, is unequivocally unsuited to a *great* extent for modern times. It is like a pair of jeans whose owner, has gained tremendous weight and is fruitlessly squeezing himself into it. There are three alternatives to this. One, dispose of the old jeans and get a new pair, or, two, if the pair of the jean trousers holds a sentimental value, then the owner must diligently lose weight or, three, compromise to tailoring the fabric to his size.

This is where we stand regarding our ancient constitution. From presidential abuse of powers, blurred lines between the separation of powers, to electronic wiretapping by the National Security Agency—in a new era when the definition of privacy has changed profoundly, the government and its people are constantly squeezing themselves into an outfitted pair of jeans. Hence, from this, we see bizarre constitutional interpretations by the Courts, "judicial reviews," "signing statements" by presidents, weird legislation in Congress; bending and twisting of the law by the federal government and the states' government, too. And there are many Americans whose rights and concerns do not fit clearly within the framework of our constitution. American civil law in practice is compromised.

This challenge is a great impediment to addressing the confusions over the Second Amendment. The whole scheme needs rigorous and practical re-evaluation.

The integrity of the constitution

"I believe in the constitution" is a cliché some often assert religiously. Usually, these are partisan hacks. They stand at the edge ofgt deifying the document. However, while its indirect acclaim of deity is an exaggeration, the document is a *living thing* in a social sense, rather than a biological sense. It is, because it constitutes a set of laws that should, and are indeed keeping up with the times, howbeit, at a pace that is too slow.

The Founders' have designed the constitution this way—so that it is difficult to amend—to maintain not only a stable form of government, but also, a steady form of *governing*. This is logical. A just and consistent and flexible legal framework of a state is a *sine qua non* for a stable state where freedom, and also importantly, a great social order can flourish. Hence, government once established will not be "…altered or changed for light or transient causes…" This applies to the socio-political stability in the country, too.

But when it is self-defeating and it is abhorrent to the liberty of some or threatens that of others, then it is only common sense to alter it and institute a practical one that, in the best way, guarantees the preservation of life, liberty, security, and self-determinism.

As time progresses, the history of civilization has shown that with time, the most liberal forms of laws may become despotic or "barbarous" as new ideals of what constitutes liberty evolve and outpace the codes of law.

There may be an inherent integrity of the constitution, it is however not infallible. History has shown that. And those who dismiss the inerrancy or insufficient conformity of the constitution to moral law are not unpatriotic. Too, from distant history to date, this fact is indisputable: the government itself is not infallible, neither is the legal framework under which the government and its people are bound.

America's understanding of the Second Amendment, or the blanket and broad use of it, violates natural law. That said, the provision, if understood clearly, and applied wisely, virtue may prevail over savagery.

On the other hand, if not understood, and its wise application is impossible, then the provision needs to be abolished with an option for a replacement of a similar amendment that carries no ambiguousness and gives no room for loopholes by any jurisdiction within the United States.

There has been a nuisance attached to this sacrosanct heritage of ours: The Prohibition and the anti- or counter-Prohibition amendments. So, if these nuisances blot the US Constitution, why can't the nation rally around a legitimate issue that confronts civilization—literally, a matter of life and death?

The constitution is a document that was ordained in the consummation of creating a more perfect union—on the promise and premise of a work that *will* be in progress. And the document was made amenable to doing just that, as again, the ratification of the amendments enumerated in the Bill of Rights soon after its adoption, demonstrated. Fidelity to the preamble—the statement of purpose— of the constitution stringently inculpates all civilians—*the people*, both the government and the governed, and exculpates none, to see to the fulfillment of "domestic tranquility" among its many goals and to push for a more perfect Republic.

A CRITICAL MILITIA

Is there a militia in need of regulation?

Yes, there is: the ACPD: America's Cities' Police Departments. The police fit the definition of what a militia is, and, it therefore subject to regulation. No entity should self-regulate—if it does so, fair regulation is farfetched.

The police departments of many American cities are becoming increasingly militarized: with tanks, sophisticated weaponry, and military-style law enforcement on American streets,

If there is a Geneva convention that governs international conduct of battle, United States military field manual that regulates its uniformed personnel in combat, the lack potent federal police regulation and oversight is a mischaracterization of the republican structure of the United States as a nation.

This of no doubt contributes to the excessive use of force by the police department of some cities and the disproportionate use of unfair—if not outright illegal—lethal force against minority groups.

And while the cities and states in which these police departments maintain jurisdiction may maintain regulatory powers, and some, enforce them frequently, recent events have shown that this total local approach has fallen short.

The SCOTUS perhaps *directly* or *indirectly* as anyone may present the argument, regulated the national law enforcement conduct—mostly, the men of arms, when the Court declared that suspects in custody of law enforcement officers should be *Mirandized*.

The Miranda Right is an imposition of regulation upon the militia of the different towns', cities', and national armed law enforcement officers.

Certainly, a blanket national regulation for the police is altogether impractical as New York City, Dallas, and Fargo police departments all face different challenges. But as militias, having failed the test of the "Republican" experiment, it is the responsibility of the federal government's justice apparatus to impose some rigorous guidelines with potent teeth upon them with room for flexibilities to deal with the differential challenges that face different local authorities due to their societal structures.

In fact, one may argue that the factor of "societal structure" itself warrants such regulation. Many of the crises encumbering American law enforcement is predicated upon enforcing the law in regions—mostly cities—with high population and/or high population density. And urban law enforcement is to a great extent, complicated by diversity and its social complexities such as socioeconomic, sociopolitical, and cultural uniqueness among different groups—sometimes created by *de facto* segregation—races, ethnicities, and religious groups.

To ameliorate these, both for the citizenry, the local government official, and the law enforcement agent, the panacea seems to be implementing some systematic umbrella of regulation of the *militia* of our local *cities, towns, municipalities,* and *hamlets.* The sovereignty of our local government under the banner of one Republic will be a hotly contested issue in this regard.

But the ultimate regulation that can keep America's police ethically holy is not regulating *only* the force itself, but regulating the armament of the populace over which they enforce the law. American police personnel, in general, are infamous for using lethal force excessively.

And they will continue to do so as long as they are enforcing the law among the most armed civilian population in the world. If the population is "less armed," or unarmed at all, then the current *modus operandi* of "America's Cities' Police Departments" will be different, and, the excessive and frequent use of lethal force will be less observed as pervasive as it is today. This is by no means an attempt to exonerate the police.

Although, this, to some extent carries the intonation of a blame on the victim of police violence. However, there is an inherent truth to this assertion.

A few bad apples?

The jovial rhetorical question "How do you like them apples?" has appeared in a couple of movies. The bad apples in this case, however, without equivocation are distasteful and grotesque.

"A few bad apples" is the characterization that many die-hard conservatives—"fans of men in blue"—use, to justify the fact the police is a force for good (which is right) and incorruptible (wrong), thus, the public scrutiny of such courageous men is unfair.

Granted, people indeed underestimate the service of the police to the country at large. While the nation's military force is a deterrence and a combating force in offense and defense against the nation's foes, police officers serve to preserve peace in the community; many, putting their lives on the line. Thus, the transgression of *one* law enforcement personnel should not be visited on the rest of their *individual* colleagues, but on the law enforcement institution itself.

It becomes counterintuitive, though, when police brutal acts then serve as a catalyst for community destabilization. Some of these "bad apples" unleash barbaric forces on civilians as though their personal problems have trailed them to work, or as a psychopathic catharsis.

Truly, the police must not be cast as the villain of the society. And naturally, it is abominable to target the lives of law enforcement—that is, the police—and perpetuate violence against that body. Events of this nature, not uncommon all over the United States, are abhorrent.

"Bad apples" (in this context) on the other hand, can be poisonous to a bushel of nutritious apples. For instance, a drop of ink can discolor a bowl of water. A thousandth of a litter vial of certain chemicals and toxins in an Olympic-sized pool (~2,500,000 liters in volume) is sufficient to make the pool lethal and dangerously poisonous.

Therefore, when few of them is bad, a great and tainting damage may be done, as it already has, and continues to be. So, "how do you like them apples?"

A CASE AGAINST DC V. HELLER
(A Succinct Argument)

To begin with, before any philosophical debates, America is traumatized: women, men and children of diverse races, religion and from different regions of the country. The homeland itself it traumatized. There is a psychological injury inflicted upon the American people by the ubiquitous savagery of firearm (mostly domestic) terrorism.

As mentioned earlier, there is little need for beating around the bush in search for precedence, history, politics of the epoch and *excess* states legal codes predating or crafted around the Bill of Rights in 1791, to bring an argument against *DC v. Heller*, which arguably, is one of the most significant firearm rulings by the Supreme Court of the United States (SCOTUS). As stated by Heller's attorney, Clark Neiley,

> America went over 200 years without knowing whether a key provision of the Bill of Rights meant anything...[45]

---

[45] See reference 2

Neily's assessment, though wrong in the light of the analyses of the SCOTUS' decision, shows the significance of the ruling.

Dick Anthony Heller had approached the National Rifle Association to overturn a District of Columbia's firearm regulation law. However, the NRA did not file the suit per se, they nevertheless, expended as much energy in stifling and ruffling the case to ensure that the decision is favorable to their terms.

The case, built-up, beginning with lower Courts, reached the Supreme Court of the United States with six plaintiffs: Shelly Parker, Tom Palmer, George Lyon, Gillian St. Lawrence, and Heller. It might have been organized as a Civil Rights strategy to parallel the drastic shifts in constitutional law throughout the history of American Civil Rights movements' landmark achievements, unchecked firearms proliferation and ownership, however, is detrimental to the fundamental civil liberties of the people of the American society.

And, though the Second Amendment is indeed a Civil Rights case, the plaintiffs, as well as the Court, have it twisted. The rationale of the case and its outcome circumvents the ideal of the safety of other Americans by its extreme protection of the unrestricted right to bear and keep arms.

The ruling created a constitutional vacuum guarantying a legal atmosphere under which states can pass preposterous gun laws, protest federal counter-legislations, all under the guise of state's right. It's almost like the infamous *Plessy v Fergusson* decision which sidestepped the Fourteenth Amendment and gave states a constitutional loophole to enact Jim Crow laws.

Besides, it incapacitates implementation of necessary regulations such as basic safety guidelines: for instance, provisions meant to protect children who can easily have access to guns of careless owners. This, unfortunately often results in deadly accidents. Sadly, toddlers and children gun violence are endemic in the United States.

Here, the Second Amendment, with such a political judicial maneuver, hands states and jurisdictions nearly a blank oversight. And most importantly, the very cradle of the constitution and a liberal society is betrayed—the fundamental liberty inherent to all lives: the inalienable right to life.

Constitutional dilemma

A critical phenomenon that Americans must come to terms with, and reject, is the bizarre extra-constitutional adjudication by the High Court: adjudications that arrest time as it was in the past, and, the use arbitrary Founder's intent or originalism. As argued before, the constitution is a living document that has to keep up with time, not the other way around.

If a measure in the constitution is unethical, it must be stricken out or amended, as it has been done twenty-seven times until this moment—2016. More so, if a constitutional provision is limited in scope fitting for its design, that provision must be expanded. If a provision is vague, and there are "loopholes" exploited by states and individuals, it *should* be clarified by legislation. And lastly, if there has to be a provision to address a rising political construct or right a societal wrong, an amendment can be proposed.

The constitutional text is malleable. It was handed down to posterity as such by those who crafted it, howbeit, tough in malleability.

The syllabus of the ruling *DC v. Heller* is an example of a train of extra-constitutional exercise of common law. It is far more complicated than the constitution itself.

In interpreting the constitution, Framer's intent, Political Journals, historical accounts, and so on are nearly, if not totally, irrelevant. If the Framers fail to put it on the parchment and endorse it with their signature, it isn't in the constitution. That is not to imply that the constitution is always just, moral, and all fulfilling, which is why it is opened modification instead of squeezing arguments into an antiquated sentence: in this case, the Second Amendment.

Granted, the constitution was crafted by an elite set of men, who in fact, wanted a Republic and a system of government which course and events are guided by the elite. Notwithstanding, the common man was still privy to his rights as of now. And, if that's not the case, the American constitution, the shortest constitution written in the English language, should not be foreign to its populace. Such is it if a syllabus of the majority and minority opinions on an amendment of one sentence is so voluminous and unwieldy that it can only be construed, for the most part, by scholars.

The DC regulatory laws challenged

According to a summary of *DC v. Heller* from Old Research Report on October 17, 2008, the principal analyst being Veronica Rose, the plaintiffs challenged several DC ordinances on firearm regulation. And the report summarizes them as thus:

- Generally banned handgun possession by making it a crime to carry unregistered guns and banning registration of guns not registered before 1976 (with an exception for D.C. law enforcement officials) (D.C. Code §§ 7-2501.01(12), 7-2502.01(a), and 7-2502.02(a)(4));
- Prohibited carrying handguns anywhere in D.C. without a license (which a police chief could issue for up to one year) (D.C. Code §§ 22-4504(a) and 22-4506); and
- Required all firearms to be stored unloaded, disassembled, or bound by a trigger lock or other similar device, unless they were located at a business place or being used for lawful recreational activities (D.C. Code § 7-2507.02).

The Case

What matters in this case, is not the applicability of Second Amendment as a statute applicable to the District of Columbia as a federal enclave or a state. (In fact, what a "*state*" constitutes is expressed in many points in this essay). Neither this nor any legal technicalities of the status of DC in the union is very much significant to the broad consequence of the decision of the SCOTUS on the case.

The relevant issue at hand is, *to what extent is regulation permitted under the constitutional provision?* The first proposition in the syllabus in the majority opinion is that one, "the Second Amendment protects an individual right to possess firearm unconnected with service in a militia..." (Pp. 2 – 53). Or did it? That is, in the wording of the Amendment and that, in connection with the definition of a militia, does that statement hold true? No, it does not.

The fourth part of the first proposition (1d) described the Second Amendment of "dubious worth" Pp 30 – 32.

It is ambiguous and relies heavily on tradition. Traditionally and historically, Americans and colonial Americans have always borne arms for self-defense, hunting, and other purposes, say, engage in a duel, which is supposedly *not* illegal.

Notwithstanding, there are many cultural phenomena not necessarily associated with the constitution—vaguely or explicitly—that became culturally integrated into society, and these were *not* illegal either.

The text of the constitution, for example, does not contain the word "slave" neither does it specify directly what race or ethnic group are to be enslaved, except that, a slave (mentioned in other technical terms) is three-fifth of a man in allotting delegation to the United States of House of Representatives from the states and the abolition of its transatlantic trade in 1808. Yet, there was slavery. And after its abolition, and the passage of the Thirteenth, Fourteenth, and Fifteenth Amendments, some form of involuntary servitude continued for a while, equality wasn't fully guaranteed hundred years later and the freedom to vote is still been stifled in the twenty-first century.

While states' constitutions preceding or immediately following the Bill of Rights may explicitly state the purpose of the right to bear arms, as Justice Stevens noted in the case of "Declaration of Rights of Vermont and Pennsylvania," that *right to self-defense*, is not specified in the US Constitution. Nationally, it is a tradition. And it is not a terrible tradition if there is regulation of what types of weapons can be used and how they should be deployed at home safely, considering the paraphernalia that constitute weapon up until the 1700s.

According to the *Washington Post* report on December 31, 2015, 265 people were accidentally shot by children in 2015. These include children who shot themselves (unintentional suicides), or worse, children who shot other children, usually siblings, and in some cases, adults, too. The number of children who have died of accidental shots from armed weapons stored at home, could have been dramatically reduced by one of the DC statutes (D.C. Code § 7-2507.02), struck down by *DC v. Heller* were it to be a federal statute, or, if other US jurisdictions implement such as a law.

In a town hall hosted by CNN, after a series of Executive Actions by the president to curtail firearm incidences, President Barack Obama argued for gun safety measures, contending that they are common sense and do not warrant overreaction from the NRA or the devotees of anti-regulatory measures. By putting in place children-lock mechanism on bottles of medications, it is only a common-sense regulatory action he argued. And these do not take away the right of the people to "bear and keep" medicines.

Therefore, whereas tradition might have it that *arms* are freely owned for self-defense, it is *positively* reasonable. In fact, it could be celebrated as a heritage—curtailed, regulated, and overseen by law. The idea is, however, not constitutionalized. That is, bearing arms is directly predicated upon *militia status*, and that militia is one which is "well regulated."

The idea that Americans have no right to armed self-defense may seem outrageous. And it is not altogether because of our constitutional right, but because of our long-held cultural heritage and tradition. It is thus understandable that right-wing activism has made many ignorant of what their "Second Amendment right" is.

Prefatory and operative clauses

As described above there is an attempt by the Court to disconnect the two clauses of the Second Amendment by its decision. This is evident in the novel definition and labeling of the clauses and an attempt to figure out the "circuitry" of the statute like an engineer attempting to dissect connections between circuits on a board.

"The Amendment's prefatory clause announces a purpose" the decision held states ((1)a Pp. 2 – 22), which "…does not limit or expand the scope of the second part, the operative clause." Two critical words in the prefatory clause that *should*, according to the Court, "not limit or expand the second part" are "regulated" and "militia." Howbeit, that clause introduces a purpose "…being well necessary for the security of a free state." Consider the Second Amendment:

> *A well regulated Militia, being necessary to the security of a free State,*
> *the right of the people to keep and bear Arms, shall not be infringed.*

CLAUSE 1, PREFATORY: *A well regulated Militia, being necessary to the security of a free State…*
CLAUSE 2, OPERATIVE: *…The right of the people to keep and bear Arms, shall not be infringed.*

A purpose may be announced by the "prefatory clause", but the *basis* for the purpose announced is either omitted, incomplete, or insufficiently provided. It is a "truncated phrase" which excludes all the rationale which the Court provided for its decision to strike down DC statutes on regulation.

Such *basis* is clear in Vermont's 1777 article XV constitutional provision. We cannot, and the Court does not have the powers, to read into the US constitution what is not there—written, amended, signed and ratified regardless of its vagueness, unless such interpretation positively brings the existing statue in consistence with time.

The purpose here is presumably "security." Which as noted, "history demonstrates that it connotes an individual right to keep and bear arms." Pp 2 – 22. However, history, while noble or infamous in its own intrinsic attributes, it is not the constitution. And this notion is one of the core principles being challenged here, the other being politics. History cannot be constitutionalized—automatically.

The reason history should be introduced into a civil discourse in this manner is that it is important to be objectively cognizant of history. This way, we make sure that certain histories do not reoccur, else should we find ourselves in the realistic déjà vu of such infamous moments.

In fact, on the other hand, history *proves* that the prevailing thoughts and ideals when the constitution was drafted, ratified and adopted, reflect old assumptions: assumptions of late 18th century and *backward*.

Also, there are traditions that are now extinct and need to stay extinct. Too, there are archaic traditions woven into history that we must see to their extinction. These are not supposed to be incorporated in the syllabi of decisions of the SCOTUS, or at least if it's done, it should be with great and painstaking care.

What is being "secured," that is, the "security of a free State" has been attempted to be explained. However, the decision here suggested that when mingled with history it connotes "self-defense."

Moreover, while the prefatory clause announces a purpose, it is said to place no limitation on the operative clause. Accordingly, *regulation* does not "limit or expand the scope" of the operative clause.

Militia is another word that is in the clause "that announces a purpose," and since this similarly does not "limit or expand the scope" of the right articulated in the operative clause, in (1)b Pp. 22 – 28 "... The prefatory clause comports with the Court's interpretation of the operative clause."

The Court, nonetheless, has a few words to say about *militia* both in terms of *history*, *politics*, and perhaps grammatical definition. In evaluating the Second Amendment in this essay, what a militia is, has been discussed. And to reiterate this, let's examine what a militia is and see if the Court upheld that standard *consistently*.

The proclaim authoritative 1760 Marchant's dictionary, described prior, defines 'militia' as thus:

> In general, denotes the body of soldiers, or those who make the profession of arms. But in a more restrained sense, it denotes the trained bands of a town or country, who arm them themselves upon a short warning, for their defense.

The implication of this definition has been elaborated to a great extent. Surprisingly, the Court itself seems to have a somewhat non-conflicting view, with the exception for "male" in its definition. But somehow, one could still make out a "one person" militia from its decision. In all of these, semantics in law matter to the uttermost extent. In fact, Court decisions have been made based on punctuation marks!

"The militia comprised of all males physically capable of acting in concert for common defense..." the decision held went further, and this is consistent with what has been defined thus far. Nevertheless, it continued (1)b Pp. 22 – 28, "The Antifederalists feared that the Federal Government would disarm the people in order to disable this citizen's militia, enabling a politicized standing army or a selected militia to rule..." This is a pure political sentiment from a historical perspective and has little or nothing to do with the constitution itself (as discussed in the section: *time, law, and morality*).

Ironically, it points to "citizen's militia" and a "selected militia." A militia being "persons acting in concert." A citizen cannot *possess* a militia like any item or paraphernalia by declaring himself a "one-man militia." Besides, a coup d'état is led by *coordination* of either military and/or militia *bodies* or other *entities*.

It is the same politics of yesteryears as of today. And politics, in any era, cannot be justified in clouding the fidelity of law. The Federalist and Antifederalist might as well have hatched out nothing less than a compromise than an ambiguous Second Amendment.

As Justice Stevens noted, there is little or no equivocation in the Commonwealth of Pennsylvania's analogue to the Second Amendment. It states thus in section XXI:

> *The right of citizens to bear arms, in defence of themselves*
> *and the State shall not be questioned.*

Here, one, the tradition of self-defense is rooted in the constitution. Two, what a state comprises of, is fully understood. Three, by the clear wording of the Pennsylvania's statute, it provides a train of words without missing links while, at the same time, not mincing them.

With the evolution of arms in the twentieth and twenty-first centuries, common sense dictates the level of sophistication of arms the government will permit its citizens to bear.

"The response" that is, to the fear of the Antifederalists, "was to deny Congress power to abridge the ancient right of individuals to keep and bear arms, so that the ideal of a citizen militia would be preserved" Pp. 22 – 28. It is that "ancient right" which influences the Enlightenment thinkers that warrant the exploration of certain subjects in this essay.

From the definition of militia as elucidated here, and what appears to be the Court's concordance with it, if citizenry militia translates into the freedom to bear arms for all, though (2) Pp 54 – 56 recognized some exceptions, then the ruling is contradictory. First, militia comprises of *males*. Today, we celebrate the fact that there is now equality, imperfect though it is. Things like "all men are created equal" is now rightly translated to "all *persons* are created equal."

So, let that be ruled out. For able-bodied females are serving in the US "standing army," the military reserves, and in the National Guard of *all* states, in the capacity many males cannot. This is just raised for argument sake.

Second, the "citizen's militia" as defined, comprised of the "able bodied"—individuals "physically capable of acting in concert for common defense." Third, if we ignore all other elements of what a militia is—a "citizen's militia," then the Court's decision as the SCOTUS held, is contradictory. In nutshell, not everyone is eligible to be designated a citizen militia. And this is not only by the virtue of age, mental health, a felony, or persons with suspicious behavior or ulterior motives.

In the states' militias and the United States military, there are many entry criteria which include age—bottom and top age cap, health, fitness, criminal history, aptitude test and so on. And after all these, there is a requirement for training—training to be a soldier, training in the use of arms. From this paradigm, this limits the scope of a "citizen militia" and thus subject to regulation.

Again, to better resolve the ambiguity for this century and to reiterate further, the etymology and the history of the usage of the word "militia" needs to be considered. The Bill of Rights was certified by the then Secretary of State Thomas Jefferson (absent during the 1787 constitutional convention), in December, 1791. The Marchant's dictionary is a fitting consulting volume (referenced in pages 76 and 98) for seeking the definition of a militia. Yet, for the debate today in the 2000s, the etymology and modern definition of a militia have not deviated from all standard dictionaries.

The Militia is not, and cannot be "the People"

The fundamental opinion that the people are a militia is a distortion for a number of reasons.

1. That the American *people* are a militia, suggests that the American populace is militarized—that is, both historically at the time of the drafting of the constitution and now. While it has since culturally persisted to modern times is some form, this sentiment is wrong.

2. The *working* definition of a militia still remains the same, except, the "states militias," which is under the authority of the president of the United States, have been reorganized. From the revolutionary period—during the Revolutionary War, and wars that soon follow; also, rebellions that occurred in the United States, invariably show that a "militia" is an organized group or unit of people with the aim of peace keeping and combat. The *people* of the United States *cannot* be a militia en masse; whether divided into regiments in a thought experiment or imagined as a potential bulwark against government usurpation.

3. There *cannot* exist a one-man militia. The idea of a "lone ranger" may exist, but not a *militia*.

4. "We the *People*..." as presented in the constitution does *not* always or necessarily characterize the American populace—at

least directly. The *people* are in some sense those elected to represent the public at large. The constitution itself was drafted and ratified by a selected few: representatives. And what should be included in the constitution, or what was already included, was not subject to a public referendum. Therefore, *the people*, recognize that while they are elected or selected, they retain governmental authority over the state.

In any case, one thing is self-evident; regardless of what this "militia" is, it *must* be *well* regulated. This is reasonable because one of the tenets of a strong state is, in Max Webber's analysis, its government's ability to monopolize power and the use of force.

Observe, one of the *two* references to the militia in the Bill of Rights, a clause that describes lawful indictment of civilians and military servicemen:

> No person shall be held to answer for a capital, or otherwise infamous crime, unless on a presentment or indictment of a grand jury, except in cases arising in the land or naval forces, or *in the* [emphasis added] militia, when in actual service in time of war or public danger... —Excerpt from the Fifth Amendment

Note that the very notion and mindset of the Framers of what a militia is, is not an individual. It is impossible for a "one-man-militia" to be a member of *itself*. It is more than "as clear as a crystal," as the Amendment alluded to the military: "naval forces," [IN THE] "militia"—*a member* of the national army or national guard—*land forces*.

This militia as of the one mentioned in the Second Amendment, is a force just as the navy is, forces in which individuals serve "in times of war and public danger..." Since a "one-man-navy" is comically ridiculous, so is the notion of a "one-man-militia."

Thus, the frequent and often unjustified lethal use of force by law enforcement is partly because the populace is armed and they, therefore, have no monopoly on the use of "violence" as Weber puts it, but more appropriately, the use of force. They do not have the adequate level of domination of force to rein in anarchy to a near perfection as is seen in many parts of the developed world.

Although the Court recognizes that governmental regulation is constitutional even though the Amendment's prefatory clause, which recognizes *regulation* "…does not limit or expand the scope of the second part, the operative clause," which includes *infringement.* It referenced "state analogues." This analogous description is dangerous to assigning much power to the states beyond the scope of the constitution. It is a "bottom-up" analysis. It is a federal law that should take precedence over state laws.

There is no federal law mandating slavery. And furthermore, Jim Crow system is inconsistent with the Thirteenth – Fifteenth Amendments.

Notwithstanding, "state analogues," as in constitutional provisions such as that of the Commonwealth of Pennsylvania can be juxtaposed with that of the US Constitution's Second Amendment to simply contend that the Amendment means what it means and there isn't any need for eisegetic interpretation of it.

For instance, article XVI (article XV in the 1777 draft), the State of Vermont's constitutional provision of the freedom to bear arms states thus:

> *That the people have a right to bear arms for the defence of themselves and the State—and as standing armies in time of peace are dangerous to liberty, they ought not to be kept up; and that the military should be kept under strict subordination to and governed by the civil power.*

This, which is clearly different from the Second Amendment, has a clause that announces a clear purpose—a "prefatory clause": "*for the defence of themselves and the State*" that *limits* the scope of the "operative clause": the danger of a standing army. Hence, here, the concept of the *implication* of a militia is without equivocation: there will be no standing army in peacetime, and during conflict, the military will be subjected to civilian authority. Also, a militia will be raised from those who are already armed—under civilian authority. (It is noteworthy to mention that Vermont had declared itself a Republic at this point, and the purposes of a militia and what a state is, have been explored in this essay.)

"Prefatory" here—in Vermont's constitution—articulated a right and "announced a purpose." Also, it does more explaining. Rather than limiting or expanding the "operative" which can be said to be a constitutional philosophy, it describes the purpose of the provision.

The Vermont constitutional statute, like that of Pennsylvania, is stated with absolute clarity without abstruseness.

On the other hand, militias of states and a Republic play different roles. The brilliant thinkers who framed the Second Amendment, well aware of the state analogues, knew that a more *sophisticated* Republic needs a firmer grip on national force regardless of how limited.

[After all, one can see how the Virginian constitutional Bill of Rights worked its way into the US Constitution (most conspicuously, *the Bill for Establishing Religious Freedom* of 1786 penned by Thomas Jefferson), much influenced by Virginian delegates, mainly, James Madison's crafted US Constitution's Bill of Rights.]

Thus, the same is not true for the United States government. Unlike the Vermont Republic, a "standing army" will be kept, however, limited. A limited "standing army" American Founders may want, but the restrained militarized Republic they continued to maintain then, has now morphed into one with the strongest "standing army" in the

• • •

history of human civilization. This fact may drawback to the idea that the Second Amendment is now obsolete.

With strong law enforcement, like it is pointed to in the decision syllabus, heavily armed state militias—that is National Guards, and a United States with a military strength that the world has never seen before, display the fact *that* Enlightenment ideology, in this regard, is largely outdated. This "modern" United States military, is one which we treasure its personnel as the defenders of our way of life, our constitution and liberties from malicious states.

It is unlikely that an impenitent, unrelenting, power-hungry nixonesque leader will arise from a civilian or some military personnel that the Vermont constitution deemed *"dangerous to liberty."* Certainly, the majority of the American people idolize men and women of service and are more skeptical of civilian leadership (that is not to say that we crave military leadership).

In such a case of a potential despotic regime, consider the myriad civilian potent law enforcement agencies: the US Marshalls, the Federal Bureau of Investigation, etcetera which have successfully arrested governors, Congressmen, and federal government officials, prosecuted and jailed them.

The republican nature of the United States is almost safe-proof: from the separation of powers at the federal level, and, the relative autonomy of governments from states to cities and municipalities. The military structure of the United States does not necessarily lend itself to a strong centralized grip (i.e. the relative autonomy of the state's National Guards), except in times of domestic crisis and warring with a foreign power. And furthermore, the 19th century American Civil War has somewhat inoculated the country against liberty-threatening violent civil unrest.

On the other side of the coin, citing and giving much due deference to "state analogues" as referenced, in say, Pp. 54 – 56, encourages states' interposition between the federal government's regulatory power and the people's Civil Rights: recognition of the sanctity of a person's life, and *his* right to live it in a free society, with rights to life, limbs, and peace. More so, this gives states uncheck powers *not to regulate* and to interpret the Amendment as they see fit, and, only states and jurisdictions like DC, that attempt to withhold a blanket right to all ammunition and institute reasonable safety laws, meet opposition and are challenged to, and disrupted by the SCOTUS.

If the prefatory clause recognizes a militia as *certain* individuals, then it imposes a limit on the operative clause. And if certain regulatory "state analogues" are recognized as constitutional in some form, then, enactment of *safety measures* by other jurisdictions do not defy the Second Amendment. The extent to which the political constituency of most of the justices ruling in favor can be satisfied is a crucial element in this conflicting opinion.

The most interesting of these is the connection between the two clauses. If as the prefatory clause suggests, that "…a well-regulated militia is necessary for the security of a free state…," and what has been interpreted of the operative clause is *both* that *everyone* has a right to possess arms and that only *certain* individual meet the criteria of militia membership, then two things are wrong with this evaluation.

One, not "everyone" is "a" (or in a) *militia*. Two, as the Court addressed "it may be objected that if weapons are most useful in military service—M16 rifles and the like—may be banned, then the Second Amendment right is completely detached from the prefatory clause", which of course "does not expand or limit the scope" of the operative.

If the amendment can be twisted, the words in it cannot be ignored: "regulated," "militia," "security" and "free state," etcetera.

There is also a couple of conflicting rationale for ruling in favor of *Heller*. First, you cannot "half-regulate" the bearing and keeping arms, and, secondly, the meaning of militia cannot and should not be twisted.

One can only imagine an army of Americans with handguns when the US military is compromised. But as the Court majority believes, "...the militia at the Second Amendment ratification was the body of all citizens capable of military service, who will bring the sorts of lawful weapons they possess as home (Note the words "capable" and "lawful"). Translate that into today: that means civilians in selective service, and reserved military personnel—men and women, who are capable of military service, should own guns. And they should be ready to deploy these weapons and themselves to defend the country. However, now the country has so much sophisticated weapons and elite trained personnel (also in reserve), these noble individuals are responsible not only for the security of their individual self, but more importantly, the country and several other sovereign nations.

And since some states have a legal ban on assault, automatic and semiautomatic rifles, a distinction between civilians and military personnel and law informant agents has been set. In fact, the distinction between civilians and a military force, police force, and other law enforcement agency is legally recognized, and importantly so.

The fact that the state constitutions of Vermont and Pennsylvania are quoted here, is not to imply that it is better or supreme to the US constitution, but to portend its clarity of purpose and scope, while keeping in mind also, that a bottom-up approach of state to federal constitution is disturbing in some sense.

One may as well assert that the national constitution recognizes the need to distinguish the military from the civilians, hence, the strong emphasis of the Second Amendment on *a well regulated militia*.

Time, Law and Morality

T ime often dictates what is moral, and, what is moral tends to dictate law as time passes and new assumptions come into vogue. While the subject matter of this essay is not slavery, and the cruelty of gun violence does not necessarily equate slavery, some of the Founding Father's view of that evil, through the lens of time, law, and morality, helps shed a light on how they view the time course of the perfection of this Union.

"I believe a time will come when an opportunity will be offered to abolish this lamentable evil..." Patrick Henry quips about slavery in a letter to Robert Pleasants on January 18, 1773. "It [is] generally understood" he continues, "that not all laws are moral, and not all the attributes of morality is [sic] legal."

Judicial Activism, Originalism, and Ethics
Positive judicial activism

With these being said, laws carry an expiration date—regardless of if viewed by morality or technicality. Whether it is specified as to when they go into effect or expire, the hallmark of an expired law is the sickening symptoms that plague a society that upholds it—a sickness arising from of the continued existence of an immoral or senseless law.

This is presents in its best form, of how time, law, and morality are deeply interwoven.

Morality cannot necessarily be legislated; however, many leaders have nobly pursued framing it into law in terms of ethics. Abraham Lincoln, John F. Kennedy, and Lyndon B. Johnson did (in what can be referred to Lincolnian Democracy and Kennedy-Johnsonian Democracy which are all-inclusive, respectively—respecting the full rights of all minorities and genders, just as the previous era of democratic revolutions that have largely benefited white men alone).

Ronald Reagan and George H.W. Bush did, in the case of these men: the renunciation of the immorality of unchecked gun ownership.

While morality and law are not necessarily mutually inclusive, the question rests on the ethics of the epoch. What is the implication of morality when James Madison championed the Constitution of the United States? The fact that what underscores most of the statutes in the constitution is not specified, implies that the constitution can be interpreted as written without reading history, or perceived founders intents into it. Its statutes should be interpreted in a way that is consistent with time and circumstances, without human bias, and, with ethics as a frame of reference rather than history.

In assessing it this way, the law will be consistent with the preamble to the constitution: the very statement of its objectives, that

> We the People of the United States, in Order to form a more perfect Union, establish *Justice*, insure domestic *Tranquility*, provide for the *common defense*, promote the general *Welfare*, and secure the Blessings of *Liberty* to ourselves and our Posterity, do ordain and establish this Constitution for the United States of America. [Emphasis added].

When justice, tranquility, common defense, welfare, and the blessings of liberty are unsustainable because of time and cultural shifts, the constitution becomes obsolete.

The best way to approach constitutional law should be through the lens of this preamble. While both sides, in *Heller*, cited history in their opinions, the pressing question is, does the Second Amendment as interpreted by the SCOTUS and other US jurisdiction pass the 'preamble test'? That is, is it consistent with justice (stand-your-ground laws, for instance), public tranquility, and general welfare?

That the Second Amendment is largely or strictly applicable to the nation's military force, national guards, and law enforcement agencies, is consistent with securing the "Blessings of Liberty," "common defense" and "general welfare" of the American people.

These facts make the concept of originalism a negative form of judicial activism. Furthermore, since the constitution was largely achieved by compromise, many of the signatories were forward-looking in terms of how law and morality ought to fit. Besides Jefferson's observation, who was not a signatory, one of his missives (quoted previously) shows that time, law, and morality have an interesting relationship that is intricately significant. Patrick Henry had a similar sentiment.

In a forward-looking dispensation of constitutional law, time and morality should be framed with them. This is consistent with the objective and statement of purpose described in the Preamble to the Constitution of the United States.

The heart of judicial activism, often perpetuated by the left, is how time and morality can be squared with the law. And time often defines what is ethical. All the rulings of the 1950s onwards, in which law was brought *under* time, guaranteed full equality in civil liberties for all Americans.

Though neither slavery nor Afro-American Civil Rights are the issues being addressed here, the comments of the Founders on these, and their anticipation that morality will eventually square with the law with the passage of time necessitates discussing the aforementioned issues. The public health crisis of gun violence is as unethical as the evils of discrimination; hence, the *idea* of *time* and law are the critical factors in ensuring Civil Rights of all Americans. While gun violence is a public health crisis, it's a Civil Rights issue, too. After all, we all have the right to live.

The view of slavery with respect to time—a terrible blot on American history—can be said to be tantamount to the danger of modern sophisticated weaponry, which the Founders had myopically anticipated. So, though the barbarity of slavery cannot, and ever, equate the evil of gun violence, it is a fitting analogy to describe some of the Founders' belief that the law will catch up with time. Time being the operative and emphasized dogma this discussion.

Positive judicial activism is when jurists attempt to square time and morality into law. Practically, morality cannot be legislated or adjudicated; but, it can expand the scope of the application of constitutional statues to ensure that the blessings of life, liberty, and the pursuit of happiness will not be deprived of citizens: of citizens by the government, or, of another citizen by a citizen. These are characteristic of positive judicial activism.

This way, new assumptions will challenge old ones that are limited in guaranteeing total freedom and happiness of all citizens, and, that these assumptions will preserve the dignity and all the righteous rights of all individuals.

Politicization of the United States military
"The Antifederalists feared that the Federal Government would disarm the people in order to disable this citizen's militia, enabling a politicized standing army or a selected militia to rule..." the Court opined in its justification for its *Heller* decision.

Federalist Papers No. 8, 25, 17, 29, and 46 were referenced by the SCOTUS. However, Federalist Papers 8 and 29 speak clearly to the position of the Federalist in establishing a potent centralized military, and no Federalist Paper infers or proposes disarming the people, in fact, many of the Papers juggle how a "standing army" can be justified with the people's civil liberties. That is, how the constitution should be structured regarding the armament of the people and a "standing army" (the United States military).

Both sides of the debate may employ the Federalist Papers, the key question however is, *what ideology express therein rhymes with time?* That is, which one is proper for this era: the twenty-first century. After all, Hamilton, Madison, and John Jay, are neither living in the twenty-first century nor were they able to divine the controversies of its generation.

One Federalist opinion that the Court alleged that the Antifederalists were afraid of regarding bearing and keeping arms can be glimpsed in Federalist Paper No. 8, which authorship is attributed to Alexander Hamilton. At the heart of the article is the idea of avoiding power rivalries among states, and thus, establish deterrence against foreign aggression by maintaining a centralized Union military force.

While most of the Framers attitude towards arms are largely conservative, the question here is the *idea of the law catching up with time.* Time constantly define ethics. This cannot be emphasized enough.

If politicization of the military was the fear of the Antifederalists, then constitutionally placing the authority over the military to the president of the United States, even with the consent of Congress, is a historical error. And it is, considering that all government officials conferred with the power over the military are both civilians and politicians, and, they can use that authority to political ends.

Presidents use the military force to enforce the laws they are partial to, and, as well to preserve the status quo, if preferred. This is an instance of the military being used to achieve a political and ideological end.

● ● ●

Resistance by "the organize militia" or the "people's militia" not subject to government-sanctioned legitimacy, is illegal. And the true "militia necessary to the security of a free State" will be in place to shut down such anarchy. This is the philosophy of militancy in modern-day America. The government's right to monopolize force is superior to any idea of a non-sanctioned militia, and thus, it can regulate gun ownership as it sees fit.

In democracies, politics serve as a fundamental tool of government, and while some government officials are stubbornly ideological persons, there are pragmatic people, howbeit, rare. Politics is largely the instrument of governing in democracies. Being cognizant of this, yet, the Founders decide to place authority over the military to a political leader, styled: The Commander-in-Chief.

Time is a crucial variable in the equation of law and ethics. Yes, a *viable*. It determines the value of ethics and consequently, what should be characterized as lawful.

From the very conception of the United States, the military has been used to achieve political ends. Though the military itself as an entity is not political per sé, since the Commander-in-Chief governs with political motives, then his use of the military force will likely be in a way that fits his political agenda. George Washington used the military in a way that is disagreeable to his political opponents.

President Washington, often regarded as a non-partisan president, executed his policies consistent with the ideologies of the Federalists. The first president's use of the military, which he led himself, to suppress the Whiskey Rebellion met opposition in Thomas Jefferson who is leading the then emerging Democratic-Republican Party that will later morph into today's Democratic party.

How would General George McClellan have used the military had he won the election against Abraham Lincoln in 1864? The likely answer will to the ends of his political conviction: a cessation of the conflict, the return to slavery and preservation of the Antebellum status quo.

Therefore, we can rightly state that the Civil War is a war of ideology, from the political point of view of the president of the United States. And, talking about the American Civil War (1861–1865), the ability to keep the states together in the Union, and being able to do this with military force is a brand of the Federalists ideology that Court insists drove the Antifederalists to negotiate or implement the Second Amendment.

Enunciated in Federalist Paper No. 8, one of Alexander Hamilton's views on the structuring of the Union is for a federal military, which among many of its duties, will be a readily available tool for the federal government to keep the states in a stronger Union. So, to argue that the Federalists were out to disarm the people and that the Antifederalists are threatened by this is preposterous. After all, the ten amendments that make up the Bill of Rights cannot be ratified *without* a bipartisan effort.

The pro-administration (Federalists) held the majority in both chambers of the house when the amendment was passed.

The fact that presidents use the military for political objectives is not unique to any point in history. Besides the mentioned action by George Washington, James Polk lead the Mexican-American war based on his Doctrine of Manifest Destiny.

Lincoln, in US Congress during the war, opposed the war as unconstitutional. So, one can rightly say that the ethics of a politically driven use of the military is relative to the opinion of the Commander-in-Chief who is vested with the authority over the military and the politicians in Congress who endorse his actions. Lincoln will come to realize this during the Civil War.

President William McKinley moved towards the fulfillment of the Monroe Doctrine by driving the Spanish out of the American sphere of influence. But the Spanish-American war was fought on a different pretext, too: historians cannot deny the McKinley-Roosevelt imperialist ambitions.

In relatively recent history, President Eisenhower reluctantly used the troops of the 101st Airborne Division of the United States Army in September 1957, in Little Rock Arkansas to enforce a Court ruling (1954 *Brown v. Board of Education*). President Kennedy federalized Alabama National Guard to quell the insurrection there, and, deployed federal troops in Mississippi in October 1962 for the same reason, howbeit, more aggressively. In this case, it is Attorney General Robert F Kennedy, that seemed to be motivated by the lingering abhorrence of the status quo. Thus, in different cases, many presidents have used their authority over the military as they see fit. In fact, sometimes without the requisite consent of the Congress.

Whether it's for enforcing Court orders, suppressing domestic insurrection, or promoting actions emanating from the ideologies of interventionist and isolationism, in all of these cases, the military has been used to political ends—that is, the political convictions of the president of the United States. Andrew Jackson (a self-proclaimed Jeffersonian), after all, ignored the Supreme Court, to propel his infamous action of the orchestration of the trail of tears, using the United States Army! Did the Antifederalists fear this?

An existing military is not inconsistent with the right to bear and keep arms. One need not dig deeper, in understanding Hamilton's or the Federalists' point of view, but look into Federalist No. 8. Hamilton's *forward-looking* contention will manifest itself as the Civil War of the 1860s.

Abraham Lincoln's race to scramble to raise an army after Southern cessation and Franklin Roosevelt's similar effort to expand the meager US military upon Japanese attack on US soil and the impending two-front war: Pacific and Atlantic, eventually proved Alexander Hamilton right.

So regardless of the fear of the Antifederalists, the main goal—argument and proposition—of the Federalists is having a potent centralized standing army that will ensure a stronger Union.

Hamilton, the author of many of the Federalist Papers offered three lines of defense against foreign intrusion and internal disorder: one, strong unity of the states in the Union, two, a potent central army, and lastly the states' militia. The Union needs to be bound strongly to avoid fracture such as the South Carolina's claim of nullification and interposition under the iron fist of the ruthless President Andrew Jackson and when it *actually* seceded from the Union under the administration of a mediocre president, James Buchanan.

It is also worth noting that even in the early days of the Republic, states have threatened secession if America should declare war on Great Britain; a conflict that culminated in the 1812 British-American war. In this case, it is the New England states that threatened secession.

A very strong-armed centralized government, according to Hamilton, is to prevent such a factionalism or fracture in the Union, and the vulnerability thereof. In the progress of time since United States' 240 years of existence, the military or what was referred to as the "standing army," has always been susceptible to politicization which the Court purports to be the fear of the Antifederalist.

So, the fear of the Antifederalists, while it might have some legitimacy in the 1700s, it is now totally irrelevant without equivocation to the 21st century. Especially since such fear is not encoded into the Constitution of the United States. Thus, the ruling of the Supreme Court in the *Heller* case is a blatant extra-constitutional nonsense based on political figures in the 18th century. This form of originalism is dangerous both to morality and the blessings of a liberal Society and integrity of the law.

PEACE, ETHICS, AND LAW
Law and ethics of time

The fact that there are no "footnotes" in the constitution's statutes implies that every provision of the Bill of Rights and the constitution in general, casts a universal blanket to protect the rights and immunities of all *of* the American people. It is prejudiced people who often choose to narrowly apply it: in applying preferentially and prejudicially regarding *culture,* race, sex, and religion. The American constitution is the shortest constitution written in the English language.

Take the freedom of religion statutes for instance: the freedom to express it, Congress' lack of power to prohibit, and that "...no religious test shall ever be required as a qualification to any office or public trust under the United States"; were laws implemented to avoid the deadly religious crises in Europe which are largely sectionalism existing in the Christian community and gaining grounds in America.

Thus, though these laws, influenced by the Enlightenment movement, were targeted at Christian sectionalism and infamous "Inquisition," *all* religions now present in the United States are blanketed by those laws. This is as much as the Thirteenth to Fifteenth Amendments covered the rights of *all today*, not just the newly emancipated Americans at the end of Antebellum America. This is the progress of time and law: in terms of the law, that "justice is blind" and also, ethical.

What can we make of the then infamous Spanish Inquisition or the cruel persecutions of English Protestants who championed reformation in Britain? Also, what shall we make of some US states endorsing a religion until the passage and ratification of the Fourteenth Amendment? The common thread here is the recognition of how the prevailing ethics changed with time.

These carry the same implication of gun ownership in the United States. Guns, guns, and guns! The way Hamilton, Henry, Jefferson, and Adams (not the constitution) etcetera, viewed people's possession of arms is "barbarous" as Jefferson said: both detrimental and objectionable for this *time*.

The argument here is not that the Founders are against weapon ownership by the public (in fact, they are very conservative about it); it is that the Second Amendment is being misinterpreted. The Antifederalists' fear that the Court employed in justifying its opinion is wrong. More so, a 1791 amendment, even if its current interpretation holds true, is outdated for this era. Shall we hold ourselves hostage to a nearly 230-year old law, even if it indeed means that individual gun ownership is not subjected to regulation, even limited regulations? Even if it means that people are dying, and we have a very dangerous public health crisis?

As Justice Breyer noted,

> … That the District law impacts self-defense merely raises questions about the law's constitutionality. But to answer the questions that are raised (that is, to see whether the statute is unconstitutional) requires us to focus on practicalities, the statute's rationale, the problems that called it into being, …

The operative word here being "practicalities." By historic account and modern interpretation of the constitution, the Supreme Court is fitting a square peg in a round hole, and this is very disturbing.

National Tranquility, Freedom, and a Potent Militia
Peace and Militia

While exploring the Federalist Papers is less relevant to the case of dispelling the idea that a "militia is a person" or if we have twenty-first-century "Antifederalists" and nervous eighteenth-century Antifederalists, the few Federalist Papers briefly explored here, are

• • •

meant to refute the Court's opinion of the Antifederalist "fears." Alexander Hamilton, the champion of the Federalist party and President Washington's "prime minister," was not advocating for the abolition of the tradition of weapon ownership, which the Court, in *Heller* case, described as an "ancient right." He is, however, arguing for a formidable centralized military. He is in fact, like many of the Founders, staunchly conservative on the idea of defending those "ancient rights."

More so, he disparages those who feel that a formidable US military is unnecessary in Federalist No. 29. For instance, the Antifederalist Republican-Democratic party member, Rep. Elbridge Gerry of Massachusetts in his comment recorded in the Annals of Congress 750, August 17, 1789, declared: "what, sir," he argued rhetorically, "is the use of a militia?" He continued by contending that:

> It is to prevent the establishment of a standing army,
> the bane of liberty... Whenever Governments mean
> to invade the rights and liberties of the people, they
> always attempt to destroy the militia, in order to raise
> an army upon their ruins.

The Supreme Court syllabus referenced the "Federalists" or "Federalist Papers" about ten times, opening the syllabus by arguing that "The Antifederalists feared that the Federal Government would disarm the people in order to disable this citizen's militia, enabling a politicized standing army or a selected militia to rule..." The federal government, at the time of the ratification of the Bill of Rights, was largely under the control of the Federalists in both chambers of Congress and the executive branch.

Discussing the "Federalist" references in the syllabus is "much ado without nothing." The contention here is that the Antifederalists' fears were a phantom design by the Supreme Court, and the Antifederalists of then were largely arguing against a "standing army"—something the Republicans in all the branches of government (including SCOTUS) are now hawkish about. The Republican-Democratic Party, also known as the Antifederalist Party, may indeed have reservations of Hamilton's idea of a potent centralized military, however, does the fear of the Antifederalists find its way into the constitution? Or, is the Supreme Court *Heller* ruling based on the sentiments of the Antifederalists, or, what the Court can possibly divine from the Antifederalists' position?

The answer to this seems to be "yes." Among his many attempts to dispel critics, "The airy phantoms that flit before the distempered imaginations of some of its adversaries" Hamilton bemoaned at the opposition of centralized army and a constitution endorsing it, "would quickly give place to the more substantial forms of dangers, real, certain, and formidable" (Federalist No. 8). In other words, Gerry harbors a faulty perception of a militia.

There is no doubt that most of the Founders, if not all, are adamantly conservative on the issue of gun possession. "I ask who are the militia?" George Mason announced in his address to the Virginia Ratifying Convention, on June 4, 1788, "*they* [emphasis added] consist now of the whole people, except a few public officers." This statement is quite confusing. Regardless, that sentiment did not make it to the constitution. A "Founding Father" is neither a deity nor a prophet.

Even if Mason's rhetoric is rational, it is not suited for this time and era. The Founders had no AK-47, M16, AR-15, pistols that serve as small killing machines. All these weapons are sort of a form of mass destruction devices considering the amount of causality they can wreck in seconds.

The crises of this century are urban violence, suburban "stand-your-grounders" and cults. Guns do more harms to humans than to animals to be hunted and "bull's eye" recreational activities.

• • •

The circumstances of the time at the ratification of the Second Amendment, are far removed from the sociopolitical, socioeconomic, and sociocultural realities of this time. Thus, the 'time-conscious' jurist, Justice Breyer places his opinion in the context of modern practicalities. After all, "ancient rights" are ancient. As he noted,

> I conclude that the District's statute properly seeks to further the sort of life-preserving and public-safety interests that the Court has called "compelling."

An important thing to be noted is, even if the Federalist Papers are conflicting on the idea of militia, whether there should be a centralized robust army and/or militia under the control of the states, and even if the "Antifederalist indeed feared the federal government" on what it might do with men in arms: the truth is, that fear is put at bay. Or perhaps, that fear has turned into a gleeful acceptance and pride from both sides of the isle, as the United States *now* maintain the strongest military force in the history of human civilization. So, point proven.

Peace, militia, and the fear of the federal government
"The Antifederalists feared that the Federal Government would disarm the people in order to disable this citizen's militia, enabling a politicized standing army or a selected militia to rule..." the majority argues in the syllabus. The federal government, however, at the time of the ratification and certification of the Bill of Rights is largely Federalist, or proadministration as they are also known.

Thus, first, the Amendment which passed a few years after the publishing of some of the Federalists Papers, could not have been possible without the Federalist's endorsement. Second, whatever "type" of militia the federal government deemed a legitimate is one that is well regulated, under civilian control, and necessary for the defense of the country and maintaining internal peace. As noted by Hamilton,

> The power of regulating the militia, and of commanding its services in times of insurrection and invasion are natural incidents to the duties of superintending the common defense, and of watching over the internal peace of the Confederacy. (Federalist Paper No. 29)

In other words, peace must be maintained internally by an active militia. Although Hamilton contended that the army is a necessary evil, in that it may indeed pose a threat to liberty, however, it is ironically necessary for the defense of that liberty by the virtue of serving as a bulwark against external marauders that may prey upon the liberty of the people.

More so, it is necessary for the preservation of peace in the Union in times of insurrection. The federal government in 1791, was not in favor of disarming the people per sé, no. Nevertheless, the Federalists contended that *a* constitutionalized militia—legitimate and "well regulated"—is indispensable.

The federal government's military ill-preparedness for the war of 1812, the Civil War, World War I, and World War II, justifies the fact that the constitution needs to endorse an active military to maintain peace. A military meant to preserve peace within the Union and to protect the Union against foreign agents, that will otherwise compromise or jeopardize the peace and civil liberties of Americans.

Nonetheless, as argued, a "people's militia" is impractical. If there is no "standing army" and citizens have to be recruited in times of war, the ability to wage war becomes difficult. Among many reasons, as noted in one of the Federalists' Papers, citizens cannot be gathered to have regular drills; this will impose an inconvenience on their personal lives and occupations. This inadequate preparedness consequently becomes a calamity in times of war.

• • •

More so, the forward-looking Founder, Hamilton, noted that a federalized military—though, the states maintain the right to keep a militia (National Guard)—under the authority of the United States government is needed to maintain the integrity of the Union. The Civil War will prove him right. Alexander Hamilton noted that,

> It requires no skill in the science of war to discern that uniformity in the organization and discipline of the militia would be attended with the most beneficial effects… This desirable uniformity can only be accomplished by confiding the regulation of the militia to the direction of the national authority… Federalist No. 29

Having an established *well-regulated* militia necessary for the defense of a *free* state under the civilian rule, as the federal government should, dispels the Court's claim of the fear of the Antifederalists. One of the so-called "fears" of the Antifederalists, is that a US "standing army," under the chief executive might pose a danger to liberty reminiscent of European monarchy. But Hamilton proposed state "militias," too. And his reasoning, even if it stoked fears in the hearts of the Antifederalists of yore, is almost universally accepted *today* to be the most logical.

The fact is, the same people who tout the "fears" of the Antifederalist are in strong support of a "unitary executive theory" and continual expansion of the world's most powerful military. They are the military hawks; both in Congress, the SCOTUS, and the executive. So, what is it to fear *today*? When we are within the fortress of an "immense army" under a civilian government and also, with states having within their control formidable National Guards? Why do civilians need more guns—especially military grade weapons? Even military personnel deployed on US soil have endured mass shooting from civilians and its disturbed members.

Regardless of the conservatism of the Founders, the use of militia must be founded on legitimacy and for organized security. So far, the use of weapons in America is becoming less for self-defense, recreation, and hunting. It is a weapon for the perpetuation of domestic terrorism

If the military is meant to preserve peace and liberty, today's society places the ancient ideology that promulgates "that fear" at rest. Rather, there is the modern sophisticated weaponry *in the wrong hands* that presents a danger to the tranquility of the society. To argue for more guns amidst the chaos of these present shootings is reminiscent of treating an ingested poison with more poison rather than an antidote. It is advocating anarchy and societal disorder and danger to life and limb.

THE DILEMMA OF THE DATA:
AN EPILOGUE

W hen I started this essay, I included "The Data" as a section of it. However, it proved challenging given the frequency of mass shooting. There is always a new development faster than I can type. In the opening, I'd pointed to the shooting in Oregon, which I deliberately refuse to revise to show the pain and dilemma I face in the discussing data.

Then there is the question: why write it? It is known to all. Nonetheless, perhaps, some may not know the gravity of the epidemic at hand without talking about it, and without surprise, God forbid, another shooting rampage or set of shootings might have occurred before wrapping up this section or before this book gets into your hands, the reader. Therefore, I decided to put it down in form of an arbitrary epilogue.

I began with the premise that this is the "Sandy Hook" age. I still maintained that. I conceived the fundamental philosophical ideals set fort here up to 2008 prior to the ruling of *DC v, Heller.* As of today, after months of hiatus from this work, I returned on Monday, June 13,

2016, shortly after the deadliest massacre in the history of the United States in Orlando, Florida.

Over the course of this essay, I discussed how cities like Chicago would be failed states if they were to be small independent and sovereign nations. Chicago by population, and in some cases by economy, is larger than states like Iceland, Cyprus, Luxembourg, Djibouti, Monaco, Guyana, to name a few.

Mass massacre and killings are now, nonetheless, a norm in the United States. Barack Obama, president of the United States when this book began and, hopefully, finished, has as of this point, according to USA Today, given 14 speeches in response to 14 mass shootings in the nearly eight years of his presidency. Mass shootings in church, schools—for both the youthful and the children barely off their mothers' bosoms, synagogue, movie theatre, military installations, outdoor events etcetera.

The worst mass shooting in the history of our industrialized and "first-world" country to the North was in 1989.

On December 6, 1989, in École Polytechnique, 14 people were killed and another 14 injured. Since then, the frequency of mass shooting has been significantly low and such events are rear. All subsequent occurrences have been in single digits.

One may argue that Canadian population is about the same as California's. But the firearms violence in California is no match for Canada, which population is densely spread across the US border: Ottawa, Montréal, Ontario, Vancouver, etcetera.

Again, we live in the Sandy Hook age. And like I wrote, in the introduction,

> *...the Sandy Hook issue poured the blood of juveniles at the feet of the government, and the government neither found it grotesque nor sacred as it ought to, refusing to mop it.*

• • •

Mass Massacre in the Sandy Hook Age and Fire Arms

Firearms violence is not unique to the Sandy Hook age, however, the event at Sandy Hook ushers in a new epoch defined by trauma on young children, adults with or without children. This is a nation that should be ashamed of itself being incapacitated to confront its conscience; and, a nation that is fast losing the reverence of the world despite its intimidating military hardware in the blue waters and on foreign lands.

President James Earl Carter on July 15, 1979, gave an Oval Office address now known as the "Crisis of Confidence" or "Malaise" speech. The speech that was delivered amidst the energy crisis of the time, the beleaguered president mentioned:

> "I want to talk to you right now about a fundamental threat to American democracy... I do not refer to the outward strength of America, a nation that is at peace tonight everywhere in the world, with unmatched economic power and military might..."

Looking back, today, peace and America are almost mutually exclusive. even President's Reagan's "shining city on a hill"—his view of America—is a country wrought with chaos, bloodshed, a violence that, in many areas, resembles a war zone with guerrilla insurgency.

There is a deadly shadow in Reagan's "shining city on the hill."

A favorite line of mine in the movie *American President*, is when the actor Michael Douglass' character, President Andrew Shepherd, told someone (perhaps a governor) over the phone: "does the NRA have videotapes of you playing golf with Satan?" This seems to be the case with the politicians in Congress. In fact, the NRA and some politicians, simply indulge a habit of playing golf with Satan, with the NRA storing criminalizing tapes of those "leisure times"—with

Satan. And those who are not in NRA's pocket—or shall we say—not blacklisted are simply rendered impotent to do anything about it.

> Therefore, (to reiterate this) the NRA and [their interests], by the virtue of the immensity of [their] political power and leverage, [have] hijacked the machinery of *the government of the people, by the people and for the people.*

Speaking on gun control in a town hall meeting moderated by PBS Gwen Ifill in Elkhart, Indiana on Wednesday, June 1st, 2016, President Barack Obama voiced his frustration with National Riffle's Association. This concern came eleven days before the worst mass shooting in the history of the United States, and yet, this unfortunate event will not make NRA, nor the politicians in their pocket by will or ideology, relent.

"I've got people who we know have been on ISIL websites living here in the United States—US citizens—and we are allowed to put them on a no-fly list when it comes to airlines." The president frustratingly asserted, "But" he continues, "*because* of the National Riffle's Association, I *cannot* prohibit those people from buying a gun" [Emphasis added].

How about the Courts, such as the SCOTUS, that the president of United States is constitutionally obligated to fill its vacancies? Could his attempt to do that be blocked by the NRA simply because his appointees may fail the NRA test of confidence? Actually, yes.

When the fiery conservative justice Antonin Scalia died on February 13, 2016, many anticipated a political brouhaha that is about to unfold. The ideological balance of the High Court is about to be shifted for a generation or so, and the Republican-dominated Senate, which must consent to the Democratic president's nominee, was not going to give in without a fight.

On Wednesday, March 16, 2016, after much anticipation and predictions, President Barack Obama named the chief justice of US Court of Appeals of DC Circuit, Merrick Garland, to take the vacant seat of Associate Justice of the SCOTUS, Antonin Scalia. There was much spectacle.

Senate Majority Leader, Mitch McConnell will not allow a hearing. Not in an election year. There is a "Biden rule" or so-called "election year rule" that circumvents the Article 2 constitutional obligation of the elected president of the United States who is still in office. But these are less baffling.

What was confounding being that, the Senate Majority leader who blocked the Senate's consent—that is the judicial hearings and a subsequent "up or down" vote for Judge Garland, publicly acknowledged why he did so. Why, or one of the "whys": the NRA.

"… Even if the Barack Obama calls him (Judge Garland) moderate, he is opposed by the NRA, he is opposed by the National Federation of Independent Business…" McConnell said after a round of questions on with Dana Bash on CNN on Sunday, March 20, 2016. NFIB sounds great, and it should be, until one understands the politics of it. But what does it have to do with the SCOTUS anyway? And Americans were numbed to the fact that McConnell is conspicuously standing in contempt of the United States' Constitution.

Is the Senate Majority leader publicly admitting that he is a puppet of the NRA or in its pockets? According to a Mother Jones report on May 1, 2013, with the country still reeling from the trauma of Sandy Hook, the NRA has (mostly) the Republicans in its pockets, with McConnell, having received donations of $55,800 between 2000 to that point from NRA and gun control hardliners. The NRA had injected the previous congressional campaign with a hefty sum of $18.6 million.

A bill introduced that was supposed to curtail another mass massacre was killed even though 90% of *the people* as of now support background check among many other measures. The lobby group with its massive franchise power prevailed. The same is the case in the wake of the Orlando massacre of June of 2016.

In a report by Scott Bixby on December 3, 2013, on Yahoo News, NRA influence on McConnell by financial "maneuvers" and legal corruption is painted as vivid as it could be.

> Senate Majority Leader Mitch McConnell (R-KY) received $9,900 in direct campaign contributions from the NRA for his 2014 re-election bid—a number that doesn't include the $671,559 the organization shelled out in indirect spending to support McConnell in one of its most expensive races of the cycle.

Therefore, it is no exaggeration that the NRA is detrimental to the fundamental liberties of the people of the United States especially if the duly elected president of the United States is robbed of his constitutional obligation. And also, rendered impotent as he raises an alarm to the country of a virulent infection that threatens the safety its people. And it is noteworthy to mention that the NRA is neither Congress nor a federal Court. For the NRA, McConnell will hold the constitution in contempt with no consequence.

NRA and Per Capita Franchise

There is such a thing as per capita franchise, which I describe as the average power and influence each citizen possess in a democratic society to shape government policy and hold representatives in government accountable and responsible. The fundamental core of per capital franchise (PCF) is the vote—one man, one vote, and one influence. And besides the vote, the response of the government in redressing the just grievances its people, both the majority and the minority in a liberal democracy such as the United States, is sickening.

But in an age when many lobby groups, millionaires, and billionaires are elephants and ordinary people are grasses, the franchise is skewed. The powerful—the very few powerful—have almost unrestricted power to negate the will of the majority, set their own agenda, and impose it on the nation.

They can intimidate politicians, fund their campaigns, run political advertisements on television, and prey on the gullible that their freedom is being deprived. However, how is this freedom being deprived—that is, what's the basis of the paranoia of such assumption? The government is out to strip the freedom loving populace of their Second Amendment right that the Revolutionaries fought hard to secure by banning AR-15 (once designed as a military hardware).

And as maintained in this essay, *there should exist no blur in the distinction between a civilian and a serviceman*—a serviceman who is a member of the nation's "standing army," the state "militia" that is, the national guards, and their reserves and law enforcement.

Polls after polls suggest that the American people are in favor of reasonable gun control measures. However, the interposition of the NRA demonstrates that even when the American people speak by polls, protests, and vote, it is still powerful enough to thwart and override the *preferences* of *the people*, and, impose its own agenda.

Considering different polls conducted by Quinnipiac, Gallup, Pew, and a few more in 2015, anywhere between 86 – 93% of Americans favor some form of regulatory statutes. However, Congress will not enact any measure to that effect mostly because of the dominance of the NRA.

Gun manufacturers will not relent. Conservative billionaires will stubbornly, as ironically as they claim to be freedom-minded and constitution worshipers, stand in the way of the people. Money thus can buy the franchise of the average man and woman.

An average American's letter to her senator, his congressman or president is microscopic besides the mountainous voice of the chairman of the NRA, one lobbyist, or a super wealthy individual who can afford to purchase a wheel, locomotive or fuel in the United States government apparatus.

Thus, in the twenty-first century, what the American Revolution was *actually* about, to secure a perfect union… in which per capita franchise would be equal: one man, one vote, one man, one voice, is defeated, all under the guise of the Second Amendment.

Dilemma of the Data

To put things in perspective, let us begin with 2016. As of Monday, June 13, 2016, which I will not update until the publication of this work, the following set of tragic statistics has gathered. On Saturday, June 11, 2016, a deranged man managed to smuggle in two firearms to an Orlando concert of a young rising star, 22-year old Christina Grimme, fatally shooting her.

On Sunday, June 12, 2016, stunningly, in the same city, a gunman ravaged a gay bar, Pulse, killing 49 people, with the said perpetrator killed in a standoff with law enforcement officers. Omar Mateen, 29, an America born New York native, is an ethnic Afghani with a declared allegiance to ISIS. The extent of his involvement with, and motivation by the terrorist group, the Islamic State of Iraq and Syria at this time is less understood. There seems to be a blur in the line between his psychological profile and religious radicalism.

As will be discussed later, he, being a terrorist, that is drawing the assumption that his unleashing of fury on homosexuals is motivated by religious extremism—a homebred terrorist, as unfortunate as it is, is a less relevant misfortune. It is less relevant than the ease with which he legally purchased semi-automatic rifles despite the fact that he has been on active FBI surveillance before.

Statistics are thrown all over the place, that they are as chaotic as the ongoing shooting crisis itself. As can be seen in this map from evertownresearch.org, according to the website, there have been at least 188 school shooting since 2013 to date. All of those schools are reported on the website.

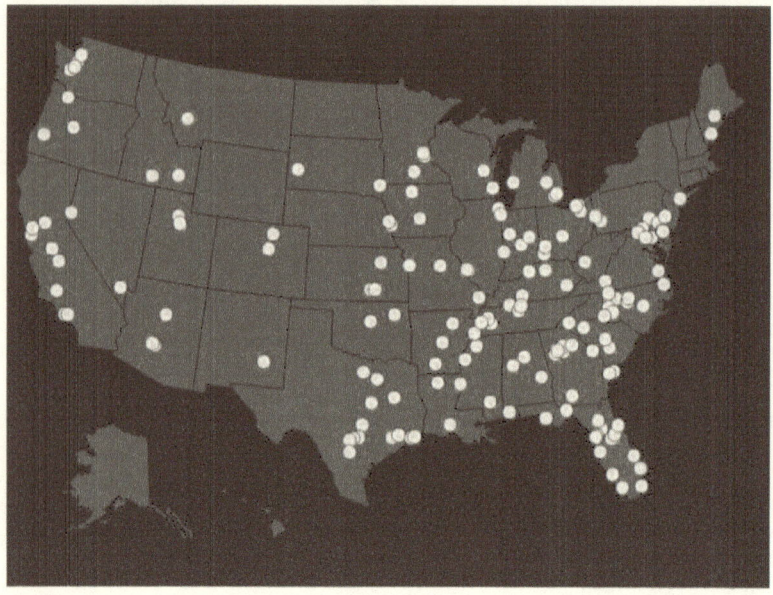

Figure 1[46]

---

[46] Distribution of the 188 school shooting incidents since 2013 across the United States. Retrieved
< https://everytownresearch.org/school-shootings> 2016

GUN VIOLENCE Archive 2016	
Total Number of Incidents	23,151
Number of Deaths[1]	5,924
Number of Injuries[1]	12,138
Number of Children (age 0-11) Killed/Injured[1]	254
Number of Teens (age 12-17) Killed/Injured[1]	1,263
Mass Shooting[2]	133
Officer Involved Incident Officer Shot/Killed[2]	145
Officer Involved Incident Perpetrator Shot/Killed[2]	367
Home Invasion[2]	973
Defensive Use[2]	711
Accidental Shooting[2]	1,043

Gun violence and crime incidents are collected/validated from 1,500 sources daily - incidents and their source data are found at the gunviolencearchive.org website.

1: Actual number of deaths and injuries
2: Number of INCIDENTS reported and verified

Numbers on this table reflect a subset of all information collected and will not add to 100% of incidents.

www.gunviolencearchive.org www.facebook.com/gunviolencearchive

Data Validated: June 12, 2016

GUN VIOLENCE Archive

Figure 2[47]

As of June 2016, as reported by Gun Violence Archive, there have been 133 mass shooting deaths in 2016. According to *The Guardian*, in an article reported on Thursday, December 10, 2015, since the Sandy Hook massacre, there have been about 90,000 gun deaths. It is

[47] A table of gun violence in 2016 (as of this date from gun violence Archive 2016): Retrieved June 19, 2016 <http://www.gunviolencearchive.org/sites/default/files/toll.png?ts=1465688172>

arguable that suicide and accidental discharges are included, yet, that is astronomical, diabolical, and grim.

Since the Sandy Hook event also, as *The Guardian* also reported, another 210,000 have suffered firearm-related injury, and there have been more than 1,000 mass shootings. The Federal Bureau of Investigation generally, as a rule of thumb, defines a mass shooting as a gun violence incident in which four or more people died, excluding the perpetrator.

As *New York Daily News* reported on Monday, December 14, 2015, 550 children under the age of 13 have died of gunshots since the Sandy Hook Elementary School tragedy that claimed the lives of 26 victims including 20 pupils, with a US child dying from gunshot every two days. Huffington Post reported this same statistic. This is alarming. Furthermore, since 1999 to that point, 6,495 children 14 years of age and under have died of firearm-related incidents as also reported by the Center for Disease Control.

Guns: Semi-Automatic Rifles

According to CNN, Omar Mir Seddique Mateen, whose egregious crime killed at least 49 people and injured at least another 53, "legally purchased a Glock pistol and a long gun." The legal purchase of firearms accounts for the same unfortunate story of the infamous ISIS-inspired couple, Syed Rizwan Farook and Tashfeen Malik who legally purchased semiautomatic rifles and wrought the terror of death on at least 14 people.

Perhaps no other weapon of mass murder in this new century America has wrought a more potent and lethal destruction than the AR-15. Fanatically religious motivated ill-willed individuals have taken undue advantage of the ease to procure this weapon as well as the disturbed and sociopaths. And any motive behind the fierce opposition to the regulation of this weapon is sadistically wrong.

● ● ●

There are variations of AR-15 rifles as modified for higher efficiency combat duty, civilian use, magazine capability, and gun size (such as length) etcetera. Nevertheless, it's too dangerous for its ubiquity in the United States. And as argued before, law enforcement in the United States is not a mediocre system in an anarchic society where every life is endangered, and everyone has to fend for himself.

The country is a stable state: stable enough to provide necessary security that does not warrant the possession of a semi-automatic rifle. More so, the structure of this Republic is unlikely to require men and women with their guns to stand up to the government, because the Republic as it stands is a bulwark against itself to tyranny.

And if anyone thinks "...the government is (or will be) destructive to [those] ends..." that is, those enumerated in the Declaration of Independence, it is already. The current political rigid gridlock of the government has hampered governing. And unfortunately, firearms are not the solution.

SEMI-AUTOMATIC GUN FACILITATED MASS SHOOTINGS

Date	Location	Killed	Wounded
06/12/2016	Orlando, FL	49	53
12/02/2015	San Bernadino, CA	14	22
10/01/2015	Roseburg, OR	9	—
06/07/2013	Santa Monica, CA	5	4
12/14/2012	Sandy Hook, CT	26	—
07/20/2012	Aurora, CO	12	70

Figure 3
The table above lists mass shootings carried out with semi-automatic rifles and sophisticated weapons, the dates (06/12 – 07/20), locations,

and casualties. Each of these events has not generated an impactful positive action from the United States government.

Global mass shootings and the United States
In 292 cases of mass shooting from 1966 – 2012, in a statistic published online by CNN on Thursday, June 16, 2016, 90 of those incidents have occurred in the United States. And in spite of the fact that the United States represents about 5% of the global population, a third of all global mass shootings have occurred within its perimeters. The chart below represents a breakdown of mass shootings in three countries (including the United States) and the rest of the world combined based on those published figures.

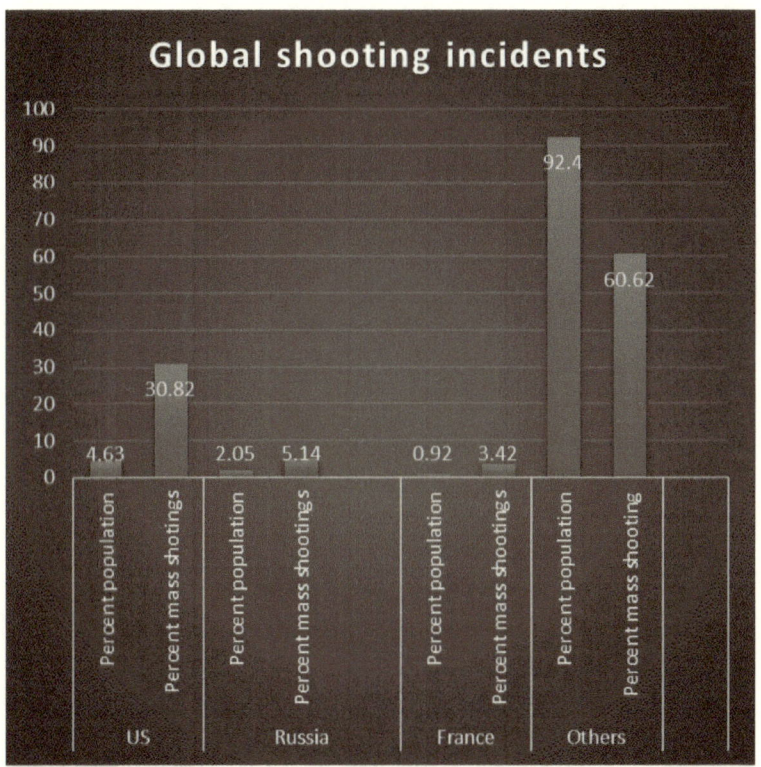

Figure 4

The graph above depicts the percentage of mass shootings of the three nations shown and the rest of the world combined. Also, the countries' share of mass shooting incidents, their percent representation per global population is also shown.

An anti-NRA push

"And I don't care how many times the NRA says it…" Says President Obama in response to the question of a supposed gun shop owner, during the Gwen Ifill moderated PBS News Hour town hall meeting in Elkhart, Indiana. "I'm about to leave office. There have been more guns sold since I have been president than just about any time in U.S. history. There are enough guns for every man, woman, and child in this country."

And, if that is translated into numbers, it's astronomical. According to the CIA's World Factbook, the United States population as of July, 2015 is estimated to be 321, 368, 864.

There are a lot of anti-gun advocates. There are lots of politicians—elected politicians—who are brave enough to serve the will of their constituencies, constituencies that stand against a cowardly society. However, these voices and advocates are impotent. This is just the status quo and the current state-of-affairs.

The forward thrust of victory for the devotees of armament should now suffer recoil.

It is high time it did.

The NRA must be counteracted with fury; with the same steadfastness and tactics they employ to have their agenda imposed on the American people by hook or crook.

President Ronald Reagan, writing an opinion editorial in *New York Times* on March 29, 1991, argued that there is a need for federal regulation that can form a tent beneath which all states can fall.

With such federal regulation in place, including waiting periods, the country will be safer he argued. "...those that have waiting periods report some success" he spoke of firearms regulatory laws in states. He continued:

> California, which has a 15-day waiting period that I supported and signed into law while Governor, stopped nearly 1,800 prohibited handgun sales in 1989. New Jersey has had a permit-to-purchase system for more than two decades. During that time, according

to the state police, more than 10,000 convicted felons have been caught trying to buy handguns. Every year, an average of 9,200[48] Americans are murdered by handguns, according to Department of Justice statistics. This does not include suicides or the tens of thousands of robberies, rapes and assaults committed with handguns.

The President almost lost his life on March 30, 1981, shortly after assuming office with his press secretary, Jim Brady, who was shot in the head and crippled for the rest of his life. President Reagan went on to write that, "This nightmare might never have happened if legislation that is before Congress now—the Brady bill—had been law back in 1981." Jim Brady will go on to champion gun control laws.

The president recognizes the potential of a federal regulation. There are progressive states and there are conservative states with a spectrum of an ideological contest that could be placed at bay by a federal law. And with a federal provision, "the safety and happiness" of all citizens can be guaranteed from firearm facilitated homicide.

On May 3, 1995, President Reagan's successor, George H. W. Bush resigned his life membership from the NRA. In his letter of resignation published in May 11, 1995, in the *New York Times* after the Oklahoma City tragedy in April 19, 1995, the former president wrote that the NRA

---

[48] Note that this excerpt was published in an article in 1991 and this number is reflective of that decade. According to Gun Violence Archives, as of 2015, 13,286 individuals died of gun violence with an average of 36 deaths a day. And as Gun Violence Archives have tracked, the year 2015 saw about 50,000 incidents of gun violence. Not all are attributed to hand guns, but the incidents of hand gun violence, or any firearms, have spiked beyond tolerance for a civilized state.

actions "...deeply offends [his] own sense of decency and honor; and it offends [his] concept of service to country."

We may take comfort in recent statistics that show the downward trend in crime and violence during the presidencies of George W. Bush and Barack Obama. Nevertheless, the casualties and frequency of firearms violence and mass shootings in the United States is intolerable and raise serious alarms.

CONCLUSION

All these been said, it is now up to us as individuals to stand up, in the character of our forbearers, and let our voice be heard. The echoes of our voices must reverberate through the halls of Congress, the chambers of the Courts, and the Executive Mansion of the president of the United States.

The NRA does not own and should neither own nor wield the power to incapacitate the *people's government* with impunity, endurance, and resiliency.

The NRA is not merely a powerful interest on behalf of those who want to defend themselves, hunt, or engage in firearm recreational activity. It is wittingly or unwittingly, a stubborn and sadistic instrument for the obstruction and perturbation of domestic tranquility.

If you start reading this book you are now holding in your hands from the beginning, it is almost a certainty that at least a child and an adult would have died from a firearm incident not related to self-defense or any justifiable cause by the time you conclude it. It's just a *usual* misfortune of unfinished lives.

As Martin Luther King, Jr. once stated, "In the end, we will remember not the words of our enemies, but the silence of our friends." If you, who are reading this text, will be silent on this issue and will take the sidelines, then, *history will hold you personally in contempt.*

On July 7, 2016, five police officers were shot by a semi-automatic rifle. This was not the first recent attack and the last as of the time of this date when this essay is being continued. I have decided not to update the table on page 135, because if I constantly update this text extensively, I may never finish it. In this essay, I have mentioned the need to regulate the police as a militia. At the same time, attack on law enforcement personnel is another route to societal anarchy and the failure of a state.

"This" is analogous, according to Dallas trauma surgeon, Brian H. Williams, MD, to a "bad movie on an endless loop" as he puts it in the aftermath of the July 7th (2016) police mass shooting in Dallas.

It is indeed a "loop." If the police differentially and prejudicially use lethal force against minorities—Americans of African ancestry for the most part, and consequently, ill-informed troubled minorities or other disgraceful individuals seek revenge, then prejudice is further engrained in the fabric of law enforcement. Society spirals into chaos. We are headed in the direction, without exaggeration, of being a failed state, perhaps even worse: a crisis of democracy.

For this reason and much more, the spirit of liberty must drive the individuals of this country, as it is our tradition of nearly two centuries and a half to demand the sanctity of *all* lives by curtailing blanket "freedom to bear and keep arms" by civilians. The inherent non-negotiable right to live transcends everything else.

Domestic, Jihadi Terrorism, and Mental Health
Domestic, Jihadi Terrorism
What is noteworthy about the Orlando massacre that claimed 49 lives and the San Bernardino shootings to which 14 lives fell victim, is

that, though the perpetrators are domestic terrorists with pledged allegiance to foreign terrorists ragtag, they procured their sophisticated weapons with ease in the United States. And with this fact on hand, unscrupulous politicians, the NRA, will not budge an inch to allow for *any* form of firearm regulation.

Shouldn't there be a regulation banning the sales of firearms to individuals on a "no-fly" list? The resistance fortified by NRA political figureheads in Congress think "no." In fact, an individual who had been under the Federal Bureau of Investigation's "conspicuous radar" was cleared to buy a sophisticated weapon, and subsequently used it to malicious and hostile ends.

Domestic terrorism is a menace to the reputation of a "free" society. What society is free when the odds of securing the blessing of life are dim? The American people have higher odds of being murdered and injured not in their own houses, but in America's "free" society. Safety is nonguaranteed in "peacetime" in a theatre, shopping mall, mart, elementary school to a college campus, church, synagogue, mosque, a gas station and so on.

Since 9/11, domestic terrorists have perpetrated most of the lethal terrorist acts on America's heartland. A fraction of those domestic terrorists has pledged allegiance to foreign mischievous and radical groups. According to the Center for Disease control, firearms deaths in the United States in 2013 was 33,636. This figure represents over ten times the number casualty of the 9/11 terror attack and nearly five times the casualties incurred by American soldiers fighting in Iraq and Afghanistan at this point.

If this were a medical pathology such as *de novo* infectious diseases, the world will be alarmed. Nonetheless, the nation—in fact, the world—should be alarmed by this train of mass shootings: it is a grave public health crisis!

As of 2016, neither foreign terrorists nor asylum seekers from volatile areas of the world have posed a threat to the American populace than a US person with unrestricted access to AR-15, short guns, pistols, semi-automatic rifles and other military grade and sophisticated firearms.

We pay homage to our troops and all others who remain vigilant while we sleep. But regardless of the number of drone strikes, targeted assassinations of foreign enemy, prolonged combat: *you*, a US citizen or US Person, are likely to die by the hands of your fellow American citizen: a domestic terrorist.

Mental Health

Mental health as in society today, already bears an unfair stigma. However, it is worth discussing respectfully when it comes to firearms debate. Nevertheless, not on par with one, the legal manufacture and sales of certain weapons grades, two, the accessibility of weapons to *everyone*—regardless of mental health status.

Mental health is often discussed as a blanketed issue: in order words, everyone with a mental health challenge is irrational and thus, incapable of many societal obligations.

If mental health should be a criterion for the possession of firearms, then what *sort* of mental health challenge, and, to what extent of its *severity*, should it be? This, however, is not an advocacy for firearm possession, but an attempt to lift the stigmatization of mental health challenges from this discourse by those who engage in it. Mental health sufferers are not to be grouped with felons, terrorists, and other people thought to have ulterior motives or unstable to possess firearms.

It should be noted that individuals with cognitive and/or intellectual disabilities or mental challenges, regardless of severity, do not all have direct access to gun purchase. In many cases, people considered competent to possess guns carelessly make it accessible, willingly or unwittingly, to such individuals. That was the case with the mastermind of the massacre at Sandy Hook.

Too, unchecked proliferation of firearms guarantees that they will fall into the wrong hands. The number of guns owned by the American people per capita is excessive to a degree of madness.

Yet, the demand and ample supply of lethal weaponry are mesmerizing considering the weapons at the disposal of the American people. They are produced, purchased, and circulated almost as innocuous electronics and home appliances.

Firearms themselves are a recipe for unhealthy mental behavior in many cases. Even people with no history of any mental health challenges whatsoever, when entrusted with a firearm, it can potentially be a lethal dose of ecstasy of death and destruction.

One may expect that this will be the case for only gang bangers, socioeconomically disadvantaged people, and juvenile delinquents. No.

It is also the case for a suburban "stand-your-grounder" who would otherwise not be a sadistic murderer when not threatened with death but feels the need to kill because an immoral law provides him with a pass.

Sometime, the *reason* of time will catch up with us if our reasoning is slow to catch up with time. And the tradition of antiquity, legitimized by law in some quarters, or deemed to be legal nationally, will be wholly and justly abolished.

While necessity is the mother of invention, as the adage goes, "invention is also the mother of necessity" as well. We've advanced on the path of time, with history behind. Nevertheless, gun manufacturers keep firearm addicts hooked on their deadly re-evolving products. The addicts being the so-called "devotees" of the Second Amendment.

IMPORTANT NOTE: TIME, TROUBLE, AND TRIALS
THE MAN WHO DIRECTS AMERICA'S POLITICAL DISCOURSE

America's narrative is now, unfortunately, overshadowed by the woeful scandalous stories, headlines, and the dwindling dignity of the office of the president of the United States held by Donald Trump. He continues to hijack the prevailing narrative of the crucial discourse of the country. And journalists keep falling under his spell.

One of the most disturbing things about Trump is, how he, as the president of the United States, is able to directly manipulate the media. Trump is not just using his trickeries to direct the country's journalistic narrative, but also, conspicuous stage-managing it. Trump pumps his ego into Fox News, for instance, applauding their "great reporting." Reinforced by the president's lavishing it with praise, they in turn, by barter worship him. Various programs on the network fall under his twitter charm and spell: Fox and Friends, Sean Hannity, and "Judge" Jeanine who rally around him while the president lauds their journalism and derides others as "fake news." By threatening to take their license away, he takes us back to John Adam's Alien and Sedition Act on steroids.

The news turnover in the face of an unprecedented train of horrendous massacres in great proportions that is terrorizing the nation is disheartening. Since Donald Trump was elected president of United States, every other issue—domestic and foreign—takes the back seat, including these virulent crises of gun violence. The media is much more interested in the scandals of Donald Trump. The news turnover—in quickly broadcasting massacres and shifting gears to political scandals—all corroborate the fact that America is losing its moral compass, and ethics have been compromised, too.

The latest news is almost invariably about Russia, collusion with the Russians, electoral scandals, and sexual harassment scandals (ironically, the Presidents' sexual crimes have been largely discarded by the media).

Yes, the heroic General Jim Clapper who has served his country most of his life, raised the red flag and warns of the mortal threat to our democracy—this is laudable, sadly, people are deaf to his outcry. Also, yes, New Jersey Senator Cory Booker is taking on the role of a modern Paul Revere, warning that, in this case rather than the British, "the Russians are coming!" This alarm seems to fall on deaf ears.

The point is, while the integrity of our democratic institutions is sacrosanct, what use is it when a citizen's right to live is not fully guaranteed?

Nevertheless, the most interesting thing is not just the turnover of the news headlines, it is the time course of the turnover. Four hundred and forty-one people were injured, and fifty-nine dead, in a spree of gunshots which marked the deadliest domestic terrorism in the United States, and, this news only gained traction only for about a week. Soon afterward entirety of the narrative turned to the scandals of Donald Trump and his associates.

The Media's obsession with the president's campaign and its dalliances with felony and treason is disheartening. Yes, there should be an outcry of threats to our democracy. However, it will, in fact, be better for them to point out that Trump's nearly 3,000,000 margin of loss of the popular vote should be the final nail hammered into the coffin of the electoral college system.

Unfortunately, if you check the dates and data of mass massacres and other gun violence in online databases that keep track of them, you will be flabbergasted by the fact that journalists have been "Trumped."

The gorilla that was shot in a Cincinnati zoo, in May 2016 because it endangered a child who wandered into its enclave, got more sympathy with many advocating harsh punishment for the child's mother. Also, a lion was shot in Africa by an American dentist, and this aroused a great deal of fury to the point of a threat to his life.

It's not so, however, when on October 01, 2017, 441 people suffered from casualties and 59 people died by the action of a man with multiple sophisticated guns in store. It's not so when the police use the body of black men for a target practice. The value of life in America is compromised. According to a *USA Today's* article on August 11, 2016,

> The United Arab Emirates, Bahamas, France, United Kingdom, Canada, New Zealand and Germany are among those urging caution to U.S.-bound travelers. The concerns include *mass shootings, police violence*, [emphasis added] anti-Muslim and anti-LGBT attitudes and the Zika virus.

These nations are not the only ones that offer travel advisories to their citizens about the danger lurking in the United States, Barbados, a predominantly black nation did the same. In a report by R. E. Guyson Mayers written in *the Barbados Advocate*:

> "Individuals traveling in the state are advised to travel with extreme CAUTION. Race, gender and color based crimes have a long history in Missouri. Missouri, home of Lloyd Gaines, Dredd Scott and the dubious distinction of the Missouri Compromise and one of the last states to loose its slaveholding past, may not be safe..."

When this sort of violence occurs, it stays on the front page of the newspapers and the main story of broadcasters for a couple of days, and after another couple of days it gets buried behind the news, and then the next couple of days, it vanishes.

If the mass shooting that occurred in Texas, killing 27 and injuring 20, on November 05, 2016, were perpetrated by a religious fanatic walking into the church shouting: Allahu Akbar! What would be the reaction of the public? Would we declare another war on terror? Or do we expand the list of banned countries whose citizens are not allowed to enter the United States unless they meet certain strict criteria? Would we deport more people; suveil American muslims and their mosques? The news and reporting turnover of this event is insanely swift!

So when? When, when, when? When are we going to have this conversation and when are we going to have it seriously without offering thoughts and prayers only? We have about 500 casualties and the news coverage of these only lasted less than a couple of weeks. This is a testament to the egregious news turnover. Soon, we're back to Paul Manafort, Carter Page, Jared Kushner, George Papadopoulos, Mike Pence, Jefferson Beauregard Sessions, and other foreign meddlers.

A shooting event that hurt 441 people and killed 59, should serve as a civil "Great Awakening": a breaking point in the history of gun violence when America rises and say, "enough is enough." Nonetheless, after an event so atrocious like this, the media is *eager* to shift the gears of American discourse to one man: Donald Trump.

While this news is worth reporting, the deadliest plague and pestilence that ravish the American society is being ignored and being relegated to the background, or, altogether out of public discourse. This is appalling.

The nation—should be concerned, the United Nations should be concerned, the world should be concerned; I should rightly assume that heaven is concerned. If we are to erect monuments to those killed in rampages of mass shootings, how many monuments would we have? And how frequently would we have them constructed?

A perilous dilemma

Writing this book has been a massive undertaking. And it may seem to you that describing this work as a "massive undertaking" either portrays this book in an exaggerated fashion or displays the lack of energy of its author. However, it is an emotional task, an undertaking so tedious with physical exhaustion.

As noted, this book began in 2013 and ended in 2016. But the manuscript of this essay, while it sits on my table or confined to my computer, as you may, multiple occurrences of gun violence continued that almost made the arrangement of this essay haphazardly. For every shooting that takes place during this time, I not only have a physical exhaustion, I fall ill: migraines and panic attacks.

I literally fall sick. It is personal, as it should be personal for every American.

While writing this note, which is largely inspired by the savage murder of 6 children and injury of another 12 in California (barely covered by the media) on November 14, 2017, marking 391st shooting in 2017, there have been multiple terrible shooting incidents. And there is no stop sign in sight to that trajectory. It is an abysmal norm.

• • •

This is one of the dilemmas of writing a book like this; not unless one can finish it in a day. What shall we make of this horrific culture?

There is that pain that this book can no longer be updated with the frequent cycle of terrible attacks, to avoid the consequence of prolonging the time it takes to wrap it up. Although finding a way to publish it is a challenge in itself, but it is daunting to have your worst fear materialize in the middle of describing it. To make it less burdensome, statistical data has been included in this section.

Again, the effort to update these calamitous events is sad and nerve wrecking. Follow the unfortunate update at http://www.gunviolencearchive.org/mass-shooting and/or https://www.massshootingtracker.org/data. The amount of coverage given to hundreds of mass murders and shootings in syndicated television news and cable news is, to put it charitably, abhorrent. The news turnover is disturbing, given the fact that Donald Trump is the narrative over deaths that are as frequent as few in a week

That another shooting *will* occur at this point is literally sickening, sad, and somber.

A

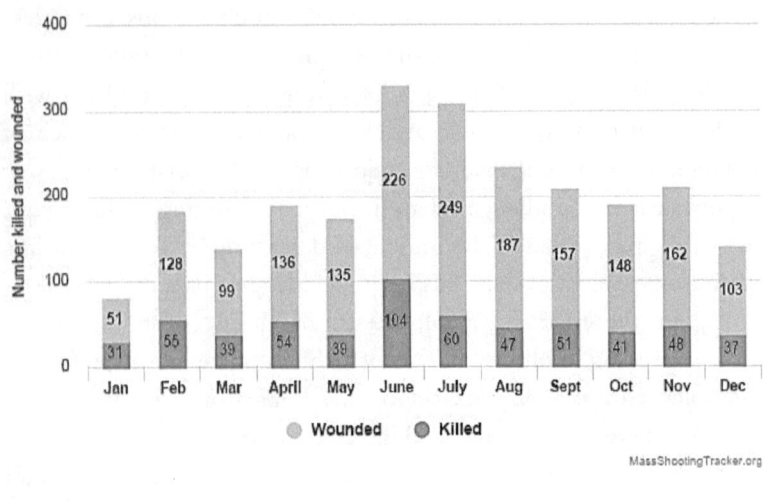

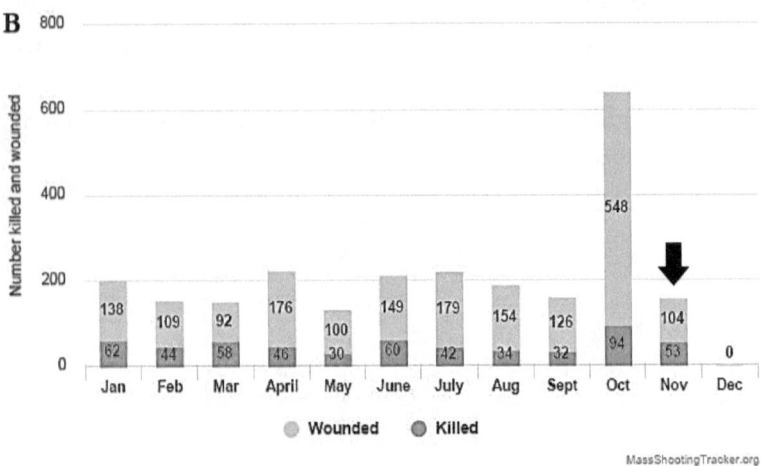

Figure 1 and 2. Bar charts displaying the statistics of gun violence, both those injured and killed. The arrow pointed to the November bar in the 2017 chart depicts the point where this "important note" is concluded (November 22, 2017). ©MST: https://www.massshootingtracker.org/data.

The Republicans are complicit

And though Republicans, as of the fall of 2017, are leaving Congress in droves, they are hypocritical—complicit in what seems to be the country's downfall.

These Republicans were aware of the danger posed by a potential Donald Trump's presidency. The jello-spined Speaker of the House of Representatives, Paul Ryan, once quipped that *anything* they could elect to the Office of the President of the United States with hands that can sign the bills placed before him will be of an advantage over Trump's opponent.

"I am a Christian, conservative and Republican, in that order" Mike Pence, vice president of the United States claimed at the 2016 Republican convention. But his so-called principled gentlemanly demeanor is an utter fasçade. He stood by his boss (Mr. Trump) in the face of multiple sexual assaults allegations. He went along the "locker room banter" assertions of his boss, and his (Trump) unconstitutional derision of journalism as "fake news" while he often cites *the National Enquirer.* At all rates, Pence CANNOT denounce his boss' misconducts. He maintains an unsympathetic attitude towards the victims of gun violence and sexual assault; and he is simply, a robotic mannequin that Trump exhibits as he sees fit.

Many of these Republican pundits, senators, and congressmen or congresswomen can now only see the danger posed by Trump to the solvency of United States in terms of America's unique foreign posture, the success of domestic policy, and the preservation of the ideals of democracy.

However, there was a time when Donald Trump's presidency could have been stopped. You need not think of the possibility of going back in time to "un-elect" Donald Trump. These Republicans are now coming out in droves in condemnation of the president, when, before the election, they could have opened their eyes and mouth and make a patriotic choice between the "lesser of two evils" of the 2016 presidential candidates.

But looking back, even during the election process, it is clear that Trump's opponent would not play chicken with the United States presidency.

"The bad hobmre doctrine" of President's Executive Orders is largely a pretext that being hospitable to certain immigrants will cause Americans harm. This Fiasco had the president talkin' and tweetin' as usual. But there are no tweets and aggressive rhetoric from the President regarding the virulence of American domestic violence: the violence that is perpetrated by Americans on their fellow Americans

If anyone thinks that America is at peace at this point, then such peace is unjust peace.

There is an unjust peace

One can hardly say that what we have in the United States at this point is peace. If we shall suppose that the social circumstances of the United States is tranquil, then such peace is an unjust peace. Abraham Lincoln, when elected president in wake of a nation's civil discord, faced an unjust peace: the peace of some at the expense of others.

And when South Carolina handed the President, by the virtue of its secession, the scepter of a king and crowned him with a sorrowful diadem; he used these judiciously regardless of its controversy, to restore peace, unity, and a new birth of freedom for all Americans.

This is consistent with the statement of purpose of the Constitution of the United States, that is, its preamble: "We the People of the United States, in Order to form a more perfect Union, establish Justice, insure domestic *Tranquility* [emphasis added] …"

As Lincoln noted during his second inaugural speech, "…with firmness in the *right*, as God gives us to see the *right*, … to do all which may achieve and cherish a *just*, and a lasting peace, among ourselves…"

[emphasis added]. This speech followed the termination of slavery in the United States.

At that point in history, the *time* has come when the evil of slavery cannot be sustained. A *just peace* is an authentic peace—a peace in which everyone shares a stake. This is lacking in America today.

It is time for the government to do everything within its power to abolish the unjust and immoral gun laws.

The manuscript of this essay, along with this note will no longer be updated as of November 22, 2017. I can only pray to God that nothing happens between now and then: that is, the aforementioned specified date. It is better to pray 'before' than 'after.' Yet, "…faith by itself, if it does not have works, is dead." James 2:17. It's time to work!

And by working—we protest, take political action, and lobby: by any righteous means.

****